RUDOLF STEINER EDUCATION

THE WALDORF SCHOOL

Francis Edmunds

RUDOLF STEINER PRESS

Previous Editions published by Rudolf Steiner Press, London
First Edition in Pharos Books (revised and enlarged), London 1979
Second Edition in Pharos Books, London 1982

Reprinted 1986
Revised 1987
Reprinted with new Foreword 1992

© Rudolf Steiner Press, Sussex 1992
ISBN 0 85440 596 8

Cover Design by Mary Giddens and Barbara Richey
Typeset by Emset, London
Printed and Bound in Great Britain by Billing and Sons Limited, Worcester

CONTENTS

FOREWORD

In Chapter Seven, 'Waldorf Education—Is It Still New?', the author, Francis Edmunds, writes: "Waldorf Education, as we have seen, came into being in 1919, that is, over two generations ago. Since then there has been the Second World War and we have have fully entered into a nuclear age. This means that the balance of life on this earth is vastly changed. Children are born and grow up in conditions that have never been more precarious and unpredictable. One symptom touching childhood most nearly lies in the widespread dissolution of the home and normal family life. In view of all this it may well be asked whether Waldorf education, from its beginning, has also changed with the times. To what extent can it still be regarded as a new art of education? What is new?" Pointing to the deeper laws of child development as illuminated by Steiner, and to the urgent need to challenge the onesided emphasis on intellectual education in our times so that children can be educated in body, soul and spirit and receive a foundation for life through their childhood schooling, he concludes this chapter by saying: "These are the guiding ideals of Waldorf education, to be cast into a practical form leading to practical results. To the extent that such ideals are realizable in service to the future and the well-being of man, we may say that Waldorf education is as new and far-reaching today as on the day that Rudolf Steiner launched it into the world."

Now, five years on from when Francis Edmunds last revised this book, this is borne out by the continuing worldwide growth and spread of the Waldorf School Movement, lately, particularly, in many young schools and teacher training courses in the Eastern European countries. Waldorf Education is now strongly represented in a recently founded European Forum for Freedom in Education, campaigning inter- nationally for independence from restricting governmental funding channels where economic power and control rule into the educational realm and its much needed reforms. Since Waldorf Schools in many countries are to date only able to operate through parent funding in the independent sectors of education, the hardship which this increasingly represents for parents and teachers slows down progress and development and still renders this education inaccessible for a majority of children. In this sense, much pioneering is urgently needed to integrate into education at large what Waldorf Education has shown in practice, especially now when everywhere deep, searching reform questions on childhood education are being asked again.

Francis Edmunds' text captures this quality of newness and pioneering. He was a master of the spoken word in his powerful and imaginative teaching over the thirty years of his Waldorf career and then at Emerson College in adult education and teacher training. From Michael Hall School, Forest Row, Sussex, the oldest and largest of the English-speaking Waldorf Schools, Francis Edmunds travelled extensively over several decades to help Waldorf schools into being in the USA, Canada, South Africa, New Zealand, Australia and later also in South America and Mexico. Back home, he founded and was for fifteen years Chairman of the Rudolf Steiner Educational Association whose members were drawn from the first six Rudolf Steiner schools in Great Britain. In addition he was Founder-Chairman of the Steiner Schools' Fellowship, the official association of the Waldorf (Steiner) Schools in Great Britain, and was always instrumental in creating an active conference exchange between Waldorf teachers of European and overseas schools. Starting in 1936, he co-directed the Michael Hall Teacher Training Course which was for many years the only Waldorf teacher training programme for the English-speaking world.

In 1962, he founded Emerson College in response to the growing need of young adults to find self-motivation and direction for their own inner and professional development. Next to the College's Foundation Year course, the Teacher Training Course as a second year professional training for Waldorf teachers was then incorporated. Trainings and research in Biodynamic Agriculture and the Flowform water designs were developed as well as artistic training and development courses in Sculpture, Speech and Drama, Music and Social Issues. In all the work arising from Steiner's view of human nature, the author, serving as Principal and guide of the College until his death in 1989, concentrated his profound experience in education.

The book introduced here is directed particularly to enquirers and parents who are seeking deeper meaning for the life and education of their children and for themselves. Drawn directly from the author's rich life and work experience, it is an authoritative and factual, yet very living account of an education which, in its practice, needs to be continually created anew by those who participate in it and carry it out. May this text continue to introduce more and more people to Waldorf Education.

Georg Locher
Emerson College, 1992.

INTRODUCTION

A brief piece of history

Waldorf education began with the founding of the first Waldorf school by Rudolf Steiner himself in Stuttgart, Germany, in September, 1919, within a year of the end of World War I. It was a time of widespread depression and much questioning about the values of education and about the social future.

Rudolf Steiner was deeply engaged with these same questions. He had been developing a treatise which he called "The Threefold Commonwealth" directed to the future. In the broadest sense it elaborated and carried into depth what had been the cry which rang out with the French Revolution: Liberty; Equality; Fraternity. Very briefly, these three terms could be described as three calls to all mankind: Liberty in the life of thought and culture generally; Equality in the social sphere where all stand equally before the law, divine and human—what he called the life of human rights, where democracy has its true place; Fraternity in economic life, freed from all egotism, where each, through his endowed gifts, is in service to his fellowmen and is, in turn, sustained by them—each for all and all for each, as the practical ideal to be striven for, freed of the present ruling egotism.

A young student of Rudolf Steiner's work was asked to present these ideas to the employees of a cigarette factory, a branch of the Waldorf Astoria Company in Stuttgart. They were much impressed. Presently some of them asked whether such ideas could not be given to the children. This was brought to the director of the factory, Emil Molt, who had actually been considering setting up a school for the children of these same employees. He, in turn, approached Rudolf Steiner, of whose work he knew, asking whether he would consider directing such a school. Rudolf Steiner agreed and selected his teachers, all people well known to him. It was to them he gave the course, *Study of Man*, and thus this new art of education was launched; hence also the name Waldorf, a name that has since gone through the world.

The school began with two hundred children, attracted pupils from other parts of Germany, and even from abroad as far away as America. It grew to a thousand pupils. Other schools sprang up in Germany, and outside Germany, in Switzerland, Holland, Great Britain, and one in New York.

Then came the Second World War. It is easily understood why these schools with their emphasis on freedom of thought and equal human rights for all were quickly suppressed under Nazi rule. The work was kept alive in the countries mentioned outside Germany, except for Holland, where the school also had to close.

After the war the schools in Germany were quickly reinstated and grew in numbers there and also outside Germany until, now, the numbers are approaching one hundred and thirty, largely promoted by parents. The problem is to find enough teachers suitably trained.

It is important to note that the schools are entirely independent of one another in all but their common cultural aims. It is in this sense only that we can speak of a Waldorf Movement, built as it is on independent local initiatives. Where there are governments giving support to private initiatives in education, these schools benefit with the rest. This has not been the case so far in Great Britain and America. In the English speaking world it is Australia and New Zealand that have given the lead in this respect. Where there is no such help forthcoming, it entails considerable sacrifices on the part of both parents and teachers—many parents are hard put to it, and the teachers are mostly grossly underpaid, but the work continues to grow all the same.

The threefold commonwealth ideas have to bide their time, but they fall quite naturally in line, as will be seen, with the phases of childhood.

Interesting encounters
What are the distinguishing features of Waldorf education? This cannot be answered, as some might expect, in a nutshell. If one were to attempt to do so, one would have to say it embraces a new view

of the whole of life, in particular of the human being in his threefold nature of body, soul and spirit and, therefore, also of the successive phases of childhood leading on to adulthood. That is saying a great deal, and yet, to the early enquirer, it would probably mean nothing at all.

Michael Hall is now over sixty years old. About fifty years ago, when still a young school, known as the New School, the teachers wondered what impression their work would make on a formal educator. Therefore, they invited a friendly inspection by the Ministry of Education. This led to a visit by several inspectors for several days. In the summing up, the leading inspector, speaking on behalf of himself and his colleagues present, said they were much impressed with what they had seen of the children, their easy yet respectful manner and the quality of their work. Then he added, ''We have seen every type of school in this country, state schools, (British) public schools, progressive schools, various private and denominational schools—the ethics may have been different but the education was essentially the same in all of them. In regard to curriculum questions for this or that aged child, we knew exactly where we were. This is the first school we have encountered in which the philosophy of the school has so far altered the customary curriculum and treatment of subjects that, to find our way, we had had each time to ask again''. They did not seem perturbed by this but only interested. At the end they recommended the teachers to wait a while longer until the upper school was better established before applying for formal recognition. It was clear from their manner that they anticipated no particular difficulty.

It was full twenty years later, after World War II, when Michael Hall, no longer the New School, was newly established in its home in Sussex, (before it had been in Streatham, London), that the teachers thought they would again ask for an inspection, before they were to be formally inspected by law—a requirement rescinded some years later. The encounter of inspectors and teachers was again one of growing cordiality. The 'recording inspector' paid a preliminary visit to feel the lie of the land, having never before visited a Waldorf school. He was a mature and far-seeing man, much experienced, serious, yet of great geniality. In a conversation during that first visit he expressed the view that what would matter most in the coming inspection would not be to examine in detail what this school did as compared with others, but much more to recognize what lived centrally in the school giving it its character and permeating every aspect of it to make a unity of the whole. He could not state in words just what this was, but he had *seen* it and he could only hope his colleagues, when they arrived, would see it too—which most remarkably they did. It can only be described, in retrospect, as a model meeting. It was not that they were lacking in criticisms, or in offering suggestions, yet, while these were to be taken seriously, they came secondary to the over-all picture they had arrived at together. Their visit resulted in a unanimous recommendation to the Ministry of Education for recognition of the school both as an efficient primary school and as a secondary school competent to prepare its students for university entrance. Indeed, they had studied the records of former students at college and later in their vocations and found these satisfactory. They were amazed that scientific notebooks could be made so beautiful and asked to take some away with them. The printed ministry report re-echoed all this in very positive terms. The recording inspector had said privately at the end, "You have set up the conditions you need for carrying out your own work, but you are also preparing what should eventually flow into the whole of public education."

These challenging times
It was not the object of either group of inspectors to delve into the philosophy underlying Waldorf education. They judged by what they saw and this led them to conclude it was a *good* school, it did good to the children.

With enquiring parents, for whom this book is primarily written, the matter is different. They are about to commit their children to a school about which they may know little or nothing. There are parents who take the school at its face value and, having placed their child, are content to wait and see how things work out. If their child is happy, there is little more they need do about it. Their problem arises when they have to explain to their relatives, friends, or the man next door, why they chose that unusual school. They may find themselves hard put to it to explain, but they get by it somehow. The others may not be too impressed by their halting, semi-articulate answers, but who knows perhaps they, too, will see it one day!

There are other parents who feel they must know before they can come to a responsible decision. They want to know something of the underlying principles, or better, the moral and spiritual grounds on which the education is based. What about religion? What is the attitude?

We hope this little book will help the first type of parents to find the words they need, and that it will provide the second type of parent with the stimulus to pursue the study further, and, in course of time, to be able, in turn, to help other new parents. Then it will not all be left to the teachers.

To begin with we need to see clearly the conditions of our time into which children are born, and then to see how this education sets out to meet them. We need to step back and take an impartial look.

We are obliged to recognize that we live in a highly intellectual age, one given over much more to theory than to genuine insight. Such theories and the practices arising from them invade the lives of the young when they are most receptive and least defensive: the younger the child, the more deep-lying the effects, inducing inhibitions or set reactions like conditioned reflexes in later years. They make not for freedom, but for unfreedom; for example, that children *know* what is good for them therefore the adults must not intervene.

Our modern, theoretical knowledge does not, in fact, reach into the true being of man. Beneath all that the average human being knows of himself, there live hopes, longings, aspirations, dreams of the might-have-been or the might yet be, unused gifts, maybe, that are urging to be realized—all these play up into conscious life from inner depths, shaping what we meet as disposition of character. They are real forces welling up from within; left unresolved they lead to the sense of frustration so often to be met both in private and in public life. There are great discontents in the world at different levels, and they make for a sick age.

We are obliged to conclude on larger issues that the present is indeed a very sick age. Witness how in this one century, not yet ended, we have had to face two global wars and all the resultant ills with which we are still contending. See the lapse into dictatorships, great and small; the drift even in the so-called democracies towards centralist controls, to the detriment of free initiatives; the unending conflicts and lesser wars on so many fronts; the ever-present menace of escalation towards unthinkable nuclear disaster. Observe the seething racial and political unrest; the disruption of countless homes, with the induced mental and moral instability in the victimized young; the increasing callousness of crime, down to the extremes of juvenile delinquency. Everywhere we live in insecurity in the present and anxiety for the future. Can this list be made to end? Even the brilliant advances in technology acccentuate new dangers and bitter rivalries—each new discovery demands an immediate counter-discovery to hold it in check. The younger generations, which means even upper school children, feel trapped in a world which belies all natural idealism—and to cap it all there is the spectral menace of unemployment, paralyzing the healthy impulse to be at work and leading to violence out of despair.

Facing all this, we turn our gaze to the tender, new-born infants, in all their innocent dependency on whoever and whatever is to greet them into this world which they must enter. They have hardly begun to use their eyes and ears when they are subjected to the deadening effects of the unreal sights and sounds of the public media; and before they have begun properly to articulate they are given computer toys to deaden the very beginnings of their original thinking faculties. All these conditions have become part of the day and we can neither avoid nor annul them. Facing all this, how can we avoid saying with Hamlet, "something is rotten in the state of Denmark."

But where shall we find the villain of the piece—where but in the mind of man himself? Somewhere our whole thinking about life is wrong and the best minds are beginning to find this out. There are two psychological demons at work. The one goads man on with extravagant visions of ever vaster accomplishments until he begins to conceive of himself as a kind of god—that is the tempter called, of old, Lucifer. The other entangles man more and more in matter, convincing him that, in fact, he is no more than the dust he is made of—that is the ancient deceiver, the father of lies, Mephistopheles, or Ahriman. He would convince us with Macbeth in his final defeat, that life is "a tale told by an idiot, full of sound and fury, signifying nothing,"—therefore sit back and do what you are told.

These are the hidden monsters, externalized in public life. How are they to be met and overcome, for the sake of the children growing up? How, for their sake, can we build for faith in a world laden with mistrust, for hope where there is so much despair, for charity of heart where there is so much enmity and hate? Are we exaggerating or describing facts? Here are the true tasks before the educator. We may not diminish the enormity of the tasks; we have to grow to meet them.

Once we have recognized the inadequacy of our modern, everyday thinking to grasp the realities of life, above all where they concern the human being most inwardly, how thin and barren it is and lacking in feeling, how shallow in moral content, we may turn with alarm to see what we are really doing to our children. We realize the more how powerfully and unrelentingly our mechanized and soulless environment works upon them. All the more do we see how an education which works for superficial results and builds on futile memorizing vitiates more than it aids the hidden potentials of childhood. It is not to be wondered at that we meet with so many negatives in the young: precocious judgement, lack of trust and belief, rejection of authority, mental and moral maladjustment, absenteeism from school, and frequent cases of delinquency and vandalism as downright protests against life as it is. "The soul," says Rudolf Steiner, "needs nourishment as well as the body." But what if there are teachers who fail to distinguish stones from bread? That may seem a very harsh statement but the negative facts are universally known and need to be accounted for. An education which fails to feed the deeper-living forces of childhood represents not only the absence of a good but becomes a source of ill. It undermines rather than builds up hope and promise for a better future. Cleverly conceived programmes we have in plenty. The intentions are good, but the generations of men do not grow stronger, and the world situation does not improve.

Some guiding thoughts

Rudolf Steiner (1861—1925) is a phenomenon of our time. His main work lies in this century. Himself trained in mathematics and science, and at the same time having also acquired a wide survey of the humanities and the arts, his main endeavour was to counter the narrow deterministic conceptions which dominate so much of modern outlook and research. He saw and addressed himself to the latent possibilities in man of advancing beyond the present-day accepted limits of cognition to an awakening by self-discipline and exercise to a knowledge of the spiritual worlds underlying outer existence.

That means that man himself properly belongs to those higher worlds. When man applies his will to an outer object, say a spade, he brings about an objective change in regard to the soil. This is a first step towards a productive garden or field. Similarly, if he learns systematically to apply his will to his own thinking as the instrument for knowledge, his thinking eventually undergoes a transformation; he no longer sees himself as the plaything of outer world processes, but his thinking becomes so far invigorated as to penetrate directly to the creative forces at work in the world—it becomes a God-thinking, a creative force itself. Through such thinking man may hope to become the active initiator of his own future instead of drifting, as he mostly does today, upon the tide of events. Rudolf Steiner's method of work calls upon man, in the highest degree, to face and outgrow himself. Then only can he hope to grow beyond the limiting circumstances which hem him in and press down so strongly upon the children.

Rudolf Steiner, by the methods he describes, was able to arrive at quite special powers of insight into human nature. Out of this insight he could then evolve a form of education addressed to the full measure of a human being in his thought, feeling and will. We, too, with his help, may arrive at a totally new conception of man—we may learn to see him as a being of body, soul and spirit, and so bring into practice an education which attends to all three, a knowledge which gives the teacher quite new possibilities of helping children towards a healthy, a harmonious, and a fruitful development of their faculties.

For one thing, we are led to quite a new appreciation of what we mean by individuality. The single human being not only fulfils a general law of nature—which might be said of any species of animal— but is seen to be a particular and irreplaceable expression of the divinely creative forces which have brought him into existence. Heredity and environment produce the necessary physical conditions, as is the case with the animal, but it is his own spirit alone which can determine the course his life is to take. This is already present from birth and gradually lights up in consciousness, beginning with the first utterance of the word 'I'. Childhood thus acquires a quite new significance when we can view it as an incarnating process which partly conforms to the laws of physical nature and partly transcends these in accordance with higher laws. We begin to see that the true nature of man lives in his *non-nature*, in that which enables him by degrees to raise himself above nature, to transform himself and the world around him. That is the being we serve as educator, but for that we must know something of the laws that rule in childhood, its state of dependency on the way to the independent, self-determining life of the adult. The richer the force of this hidden individuality in the child, the more abounding in quality is the life that ensues.

Who can account by ordinary methods for a Michaelangelo, a Shakespeare, or a Beethoven? Yet they were all three little children once and had to discover their faculties in the course of growing up. So it is in some degree in every human being. Every child is on a similar voyage of discovery and self-discovery and we, as adults, can help or hinder. Childhood is an awakening as well as a growing-up process; it leads from the 'sleep of infancy', to the 'dream of childhood', to the 'lighting-up of adolescence', to the 'responsible thinking of the adult'. The spirit we serve as parents and teachers reveals itself in a physical-material body, but it cannot be explained by the laws of physics or matter. How the modern man can arrive at a working knowledge of the spirit in terms compatible with a scientific outlook is described by Rudolf Steiner in his teaching of anthroposophy or modern spiritual science; this illumines the facts of physical-material science from a higher source. This higher source dwells in man himself; he has only to reach it.

Childhood is the shaping of the instrument for the life of the adult. In the course of childhood there are revealed, stage by stage, capacities, predispositions, also weaknesses and obstructions. By entering into these with understanding, we may, as educators, help greatly in the process leading to conscious and responsible adulthood. Just as a gardener can help his plants by bettering the conditions in which they grow, so may a teacher, by removing unfavourable influences and promoting conditions harmonious to child nature, help the individuality in each growing child the better to come to fruition. Such an intervention is the opposite of any attempt to mould the individual to a given pattern, but the aim is to do everything possible, out of an objective study of nature and human nature, to help each individual to become *more truly himself or herself*.

The object of Rudolf Steiner education is to aid children so that as men and women they may bring their powers, their own innate and sacred human qualities, to greater fulfilment. It is an education

which serves *the freedom of the human spirit*. It has been given freely
to the world. It is in the world. The distinguishing feature of a Waldorf
school lies in the endeavour to practice it.

Chapter 1

THE FIRST THREE YEARS OF CHILDHOOD
Addressed to the young mother

There must have come a moment when the mother-to-be knew, "A child is on the way." In that moment her life must have felt enwrapped by a great mystery. She may have recalled the Annunciation to Mary in the Gospel of Saint Luke. Since man is made in the image of God, it is surely not impossible to imagine that a like annunciation attends the conception of every human being. Here is a being seeming to enter the physical world by way of flesh who is himself not of the flesh. He has to bring with him something into this world but his source of being is not of this world. What, we ask of ourselves, is not of this world? Christ said, "My kingdom is not of this world." Rudolf Steiner interprets the kingdom as meaning the *I am*. The *I am* in me I cannot find anywhere in the kingdoms around me. Science attempts, in one way or another, to describe the composition or the origin of the body, but it has no access to that centre of consciousness in me out of which I utter the *I am*.

John the Baptist, and, later, Christ himself declared, "The Kingdom of Heaven is at hand." Rudolf Steiner relates this to the new event coming to mankind with the descent of Christ, the divine *I AM*, to the earth—the entry of the experience of the *I am* into the flow of human history. Until then man addressed himself to the Law which ruled from outside, for instance in the Ten Commandments, but since the coming of Christ he has learnt to seek the Law within him. It is in this light we may learn to look to the being who from other, from divine sources, seeks to enter this world through the mother. This is not commonly understood today, and therefore one thinks of a human being as derived from and belonging wholly to the physical-material outer world. One does not know how properly to welcome the being that is approaching incarnation, nor do we realize how hurtful this ignorance and misreading of the realities are to that being—what a cold, unwelcoming entry this makes for him, how the deep loneliness we experience has its origin in this. We may consider, by contrast, the picture of the Sistine Madonna and the way she bears this child down from the angel world, and how there are some down below who perceive this. Even if we receive the body of the child with gratitude and caring love, his immortal being from beyond the bounds of birth and death we do not know. But we may learn to carry this in our thought and devotion to the child in our midst. If this thought could find a home on earth, that alone could change the present condition of mankind utterly. Each mother who brings a child into the world can serve the whole of life in serving this truth in relation to her child, for truth is a heavenly seed which multiplies and the world has never had greater need of it in the hard times in which we live and in which your new-born child is to grow up.

And now the child has arrived. There it lies, as set down, the most helpless creature in creation, utterly defenceless and depending on how and where it is received, and by whom. Day and night makes no difference. It knows without a timetable when it wants its food and it knows how to cry until it gets it. Beyond that, it cannot even lift its head which is large and heavy and still, compared with the smallness of the limbs and their vigorous but undirected movements. It gazes past us into endless space or right through us, and, to all appearances, could be anybody's baby, except that the parents look to see whose features they think they recognize in that diminutive face. The mother's parental care flows out to it, almost too much at times. We know from later experience that even the tiniest babe is longing for love, but it need not be smothered in it. By later we mean that children adapt badly in life—we call them maladjusted—if there is a lack of love to greet them and welcome them into life; but also the excessive demonstration of fondness, which is often selfish in kind, can be harmful and the cause of much trouble later. Reverence for the little stranger will serve to hold the balance. But without love life cannot prosper, and at no time is this more real than from the beginning.

It is not long before things begin to happen. After about six weeks—times vary with children as they do with adults—there comes the magical moment of that first smile—but almost along with it, or very soon after, the first real tear. That smile and tear are the beginning of human language—confined to human beings alone. Darwin spent much time studying the grimaces in animal physiognomies in search of human origins being so convinced that man is derived from animal origins—a fascinating study but it led to nothing more conclusive than that animals also have emotions, likes and dislikes, advancing with desires or retreating through fear and antipathy. There is nothing to compare with the warm smile of human recognition or the depressed look' or tear at being disregarded or rejected. The smile and the tear are indeed the first rudiments of human intercourse. Laughter and tears, comedy and tragedy, run through the whole of life.

That lifting of the heavy head is the first task allotted to the little limbs, arrived at with much stressing and straining. That, too, is only a beginning. In the months that follow the recumbent little creature will be sitting upright, at first with some support but then unaided. And now it will not be long before the child is off on its exploration as a crawler, reaching out to touch (and even taste) whatever meets it on the way—the mother enjoying the spectacle but with a wary eye.

And then comes the further important stage. By an inner and irresistible urge the child is determined to raise itself upright on its own two legs, at first clinging to whatever object, living or otherwise, is there to help it, but then standing freely and alone.

It is to be noted that all this progress, generally within the compass—somewhat more or less—of a year, proceeds entirely from inner causes, and is no way promoted from outside, nor should it be.

Whoever has had the good fortune to witness the actual moment when the child stands upright for the first time on its own could scarcely have failed to experience something like a flash of triumph light up in its eye, the first overcoming of the weight of the earth through its down-pulling gravitational force. This upright stance, like the smile and the tear, distinguishes man from all other living creatures; and the child achieves this out of the promptings of its own nature, by its own inherent power of will. It gives promise that by the same human will man is destined to achieve his ultimate freedom by overcoming the world—for this will is a spiritual force transcending matter. This potential lives in every child.

A question asked is whether the child would come to the upright if there were not upright beings round it. One is reminded of the legend of Romulus and Remus, the founders of Rome, who were nurtured by a wolf. Whatever such a legend is meant to signify, it is certain that they did not derive their later uprightness from the wolf. It may be taken as a picture, among many others, to show that man did not derive his human state from the animal. Actually no figure is more upright in bearing than in our image of the Roman.

It belongs to the blindness of our time that we still perpetuate the idea that man is an animal derived from the animal. People who think that way fail to see how for the little child coming to the upright means that the whole orientation in space becomes different, the child's whole bearing is different, and that quite new faculties are born which can neither be derived from nor attributed in any way to the animal.

To maintain itself in the upright the child also has to acquire balance, and then comes the step forward and the beginning of walking. And thus, by its own efforts alone, it has achieved the mastery of the three dimensions of space. Talking to some professional gymnasts one could show that here lies the origin of their art with its command of space.

But then one could carry the matter further. We speak of an upright man, of a man of balanced judgment, of a man of courage in stepping out to something new. Our language declares the deep connection between these first elementary achievements at the dawn of a human life and these high ideals for the whole of life. The gymnasts saw clearly, some perhaps for the first time, that the physical can be the bearer of the moral, that in training the body they were also helping to build up character. One could then tell them of Bothmer gymnastics as taught in Waldorf schools—that in very truth one can begin to see the body as a temple from which all other temples have originated bearing witness to the divine.

The great achievement of the first year is to gain control of movement; of the second year, to enter into speech; in the third year, to awaken to the light of thought.

How we speak before a little child is of great importance. He enters into his mother tongue not only with his ears, but the delicate, most sensitive organ of the larynx vibrates with every sound that reaches him. We can say his larynx dances into the sounds we make, refined or coarse, and this stamps something for the whole of life, very difficult to eradicate or alter later. That, too, is why baby talk is injurious;

it may amuse the adult but not the child whose profound endeavour it is, albeit unconscious, to arrive at the finest quality of language.

Thinking begins as picture or image. We say "The light went out". A child expressed this in her own way by saying, "The light's fallen down". Here are two images conveying the same fact held as an image in the mind. Christ spoke to the multitude in pictures, in parables, for the disciples he could translate these into thoughts. The mass of the people still retained their child-like consciousness. The disciples, being more advanced, could grasp the same truths more directly in thought.

And now, in the course of the third year, a new wonder arises, the birth of the thought "I". Hitherto the child has called itself by the name others have given it—"Tom wants...Mary likes...". The thought "I", to be experienced, has to light up from within. This is the first realization of "self". Previously it was a being carried on a stream of events of which it retains no memory. Now it is *present*, a *personal* memory begins. For the rest of life all memories of the experiences will be gathered round the "I". An autobiography has begun. For the parents, too, this event brings a subtle change; they, too, will be remembered from now on. They know their child so very well, and yet, confronting the person of the "I", they can well ask, "Who is this stranger that has come to join its destiny to ours? What does he (she) ask of us?"—a question that will never be fully answered, in this life at least.

The achievements of the first three years reach beyond measure those of any other similar period. We could imagine it carries aeons of evolutionary time towards us, yet it comes with all the helplessness described earlier. It comes seeking for the loving embrace of the mother, the protective care of the father, and the conditions compatible to its tender needs. It is, as Rudolf Steiner says, wholly a sense organ, absorbing everything the environment offers good and bad into its being, and this goes, very deep, into breath and blood and body metabolism, preconditioning health or illness later. The present-day environment, taking it all in all, with its noisy, garish, hurry-skurry could scarcely be less favourable. The child needs protection from this as far as possible. It needs above all its mother. In her loving presence all is spring and sunshine. In her absence life turns to winter. How many live in a frozen life today?

With the mother there, the child can feel at home. But the years speed by! How long can this close intimacy last? How often, today, is the child placed with a care group even before the age of three? And why and when, if the mother is there, and the protective home is there with its orderly day, and the father coming and going—why, where this is possible, should the child be merged to become a member of an ad hoc company, where it can feel lost and frustrated by too much change, and variety and noisiness?

And yet, life having become what it is, with the mother having to be out working or engaged in other interests, we can be immensely thankful that there is today a widespread movement of Waldorf nurseries and kindergartens where every endeavour is made to care for each individual child, providing beauty and harmony and a wise ordering of events and occupations. Yet the peace and protection of a natural home life, at any rate up to the age of five or six, must still be deemed best.

Chapter 2

THE PRE-SCHOOL YEARS
Nursery—Kindergarten

In a Waldorf school, pre-school really does mean what the word says: no kind of formal schooling begins, no reading, writing, arithmetic or regimentation of any kind. There is an ordered life, how the children are received, how engaged in this or that activity, adequate scope for free play, there is song and movement, a gathering for a story, but all this flows along in a natural kind of way, quietly guided by those in charge but without undue emphasis or pressure of any kind. Each child is known and cared for, helped when needed, but nothing is over-accentuated. There is thus a prevailing mood of freedom in the way the children breathe and move.

Ideally all this is an extension of home. It should be in a space of its own, with open spaces around, and at least at some remove from the school proper, in no way incorporated in it—a little world apart.

The question is as to what is nursery, and what kindergarten? Are they synonymous terms or do they mean something different? The distinction is not always clear. Most Waldorf schools take children from the age of four, some from three and a half, and keep them until they are ready for school proper at six plus. This is a long span of developmental time. Experience shows that a child of five was very different when it was four. It has definitely moved on in some way. Up to the age of four or maybe four and a half, the children are still much wrapped up in themselves. Even when they are gathered in a group together, or playing together, there is not as yet a sense of the group. The grown-ups, (known by name but not yet called teachers), the other children, and all that is around, still lives for each child as part of itself. And time is always in the present—there is no real sense of time. In the picture book, the cow, the milkmaid with her pail, the ploughman in the distance, the farmer leading his horse, the bird on the tree—all this was yesterday, and is today, and will be tomorrow and all is eternally present. And so it is with all one does. It is a dream-world we are in. With the five year old and older, it is somewhat different. The children are more wakeful, more venturesome, more for trying things out alone or together, and time, too, begins to count for something; each day is its own in the round of the week and is known and awaited for what it specially brings. It is no longer the picture page that suffices but the story. There is eagerness, even impatience to turn the page to see what follows. They want the story. Each story has a beginning and sequel and an end—each story recounts a piece of destiny—a word they will not know for a long time, and yet there is a subconscious feeling for it which begins to stir. For the child of four going to school is still far off. At five and approaching six there is already a fore-sense leading towards the great step of entering into the mystery of that other world, the school. This is the step from pre-school and fortunate are the children who can experience this fully as a clear step in their lives.

All this suggests that there is adequate good reason for having the younger and the older children separate, the younger in what might really be called a nursery, and the others in a kindergarten, though there would be occasions for bringing them together. In both groups it is essentially *learning through doing*, though for the older ones this could be more accentuated, made more challenging, but far away from the head learning of reading, writing and arithmetic. To meet these three before their time is like meeting the three witches in Macbeth rather than the three benign sister fates, the true guardians upon the way.

When, then, should a child begin his actual schooling? We have mentioned six plus, but why then? In England this was always considered the right age for the child to leave the Infant School and enter the Elementary School. A Waldorf teacher might answer the why and the when by saying, "When the milk teeth begin to come away." This reference to the teeth causes surprise, but there are three main considerations to justify it.

The first is that the shedding of the milk teeth is not an isolated phenomenon. It marks a process which has been going on from birth, namely, the casting off of the inherited organism and its replacement by one that is penetrated through and through by the forces of the incarnating individuality, the same forces that will eventually shape a unique biography. It is only now, with this replacement, that the child can be said to have acquired what is its *own* body.

The second consideration confirms the first. There are twenty milk teeth. They are general in type, and are surface formed so that they come away easily. The secondary teeth are thirty two in number and are deeply rooted and permanent. Moreover they are diversified in form and function into incisors, eye teeth (canines), pre-molars and molars. Not only are the teeth themselves differentiated in this way, but the dentist knows that every set of teeth has its own character and has to be treated individually—there can be no mass production in teeth. Thus the change of teeth is a transition from the general to the particular, from the inherited to the individual, as is the case with the body as a whole. Something is arrived at which is to serve as basic for a distinct and irreplaceable character.

The third consideration is of immediate importance to the educator, and there we are specially indebted to Rudolf Steiner. It has long been understood and accepted that, except for the teeth, the organism is renewed in all its parts every seven years. The substance of the body is constantly passing away and being re-constituted, but the form is maintained. Rudolf Steiner makes a distinction between the substance and what he calls the formative forces which first created the form of the body, and all its organs, and then continues to maintain them. What then of the formative forces that shaped the teeth? Can they simply have dispersed and vanished? No, they, too, continue to function but in a more concealed or inward manner—they now work to shape the mind in the young child in a life of pictures which, as it grows older, are translated into thought.

Let us illustrate. An adult might say, "The light's gone out!" He is so intent on the thought that he passes by the image of something which has *gone out*. A child was heard to describe the same fact by saying, "Oh, the light's fallen down." It contains the same thought but the child still has the *feeling* that something, the light, has really *fallen down*. The child, in this, is recapitulating a fact of history, that an image-thinking preceded actual thinking. Christ spoke to the multitude in parables. They still had a childlike consciousness which could grasp the truth he was conveying in its picture form. For the disciples He had sometimes to translate the pictures into thoughts.

They were more advanced in that they were losing the earlier picture-consciousness, and were beginning to grasp truths directly as thoughts. If we wish young children really to understand us, we have to go the other way, to translate our thoughts back into pictures. Nursery rhymes have great truths concealed in their pictures. The little child can rejoice in them through the sounds and the rhythms. He does not ask for the meaning of "Humpty Dumpty sat on a wall, Humpty Dumpty had a great fall." The teacher knows there is an immense world of truth in the pictures. He has to work hard to capture their meaning. The children, in the main, simply live them, and are nourished by them. It is the intellectualized child who asks for confirmation that the pictures are true. The same applies to fairy tales.

The change of teeth brings with it clearly a change of consciousness, a new quality of awareness of themselves, of the teacher, and of one another. This can be seen also in the bearing of the children. They are ready to enter upon the second phase of life, the second seven-year period, to be described in the chapter that follows.

We must ask what are we doing to children when we begin to intellectualize them, for example, by teaching reading before they are ready? In the thirties of this century there was issued a Hadow Report based on a government research project. It strongly advocated that children should *not* be taught reading before the age of six; but who attends to this today? Who will recognize that premature educational demands on the child vitiate the life forces needed for further development later? It is often remarked that many children no longer know how to play. It is as though they age beyond their years so that their spontaneous child fantasy forces have begun to dry up. We have to employ adults specially trained to engage and activate them. Then, at the opposite end, in public life, we see how incapable human beings are to cope with the problems that beset them, how unable to heal the ills of present-day society—they make compromises; these delay but do not solve. Might we not consider that these conditions have their source in the early years, and what further harm do we do by exposing children to the floods of unassimilable television? Pictures? Add that today we deaden the nascent thought faculties with computer games which provide answers in an effortless way. How far do we actually wreck young lives through careless regard for what childhood actually is and what are its rightful needs?

There have been and there are noble attempts to counter this. There is the instance of the head of the education department of a large university in America. He set up an experiment which he carried on for several successive years. He selected two groups of children drawn from the same milieu. In the one group the children were taught reading by the usual methods, with its demands at the expense of the slower child. In the other group, the conditions were held more relaxed; there was a willingness to allow the children to arrive at reading in their own time. There was orderly life in the classroom— but without undue tensions. He found without question that the second group by the age of twelve outstripped the first—allowing, of course, for the individual differences there will always be. The evidence was clearly there, that each child has its own tempo and thrives best when this is allowed for, but there was little evidence that this was being taken up seriously.

We cite an opposite case. There is a theory current that, since a child's assimilative powers are stronger the younger it is, we lose inestimable learning possibilites by delay. At a large conference of teachers in Canada, one of the guest speakers, a man of public standing, enthusiastically described how a child of his had learnt to read by the age of three. This was looked on as a major achievement and was greeted with loud applause. The next guest speaker called on was a relative stranger. He remarked that the last speaker had confirmed from his own experience that such an achievement was possible. A child could be taught to read by the age of three! It seemed to him that this marked only the beginning of a process the effects of which would continue all through life, for we are not only beings in space, we also live in process of time. It is well known among psychologists that effects produced in early childhood can declare themselves quite late in life. To bring a child to read by the age of three means that we demand of it a considerable degree of mental concentration, therefore of greater wakefulness. We might say we draw it more strongly into its nerve-senses, more strongly than would normally be the case. Another way of expressing this would be to say that we produce, to that extent, a premature ageing process. It counters the liveliness of childhood behaviour and experience—we draw them away from the life of the limbs and into their heads. Might we not be inducing, through premature wakefulness, sclerotic tendencies in body, and possibly even in mind, for the years to come? This is approximately how he expressed it.

The effect was curious. There was a protracted silence followed eventually by a single clap; then others clapped; then this spread slowly through the assembly. Then, where there had been protracted silence, there was now protracted clapping, a slow and thoughtful clapping, as though people were still assimilating the implications of what they had heard.

It seemed cruel to have spoken in such flat contradiction to the previous speaker. The circumstances offered no alternative. Such questions are too serious for mere controversy. This is an extreme case of a general and widespread tendency today to intellectualize children out of accord with nature, without counting the costs. By robbing the life of childhood we are stultifying the life of adults. Each one dealing with children must decide whether this is true or not.

We are too easily given to clever theories which claim to be scientific. Education, above all for young children, must spring first and foremost from the heart. Clever heads may and do serve well but only if ruled by wise hearts.

We cannot overstress the importance of the first six or seven years of life for all the years that follow. What occurs in these years preconditions the bodily, mental and moral life, therefore also the degree of stability or instability of character to be met later. It is in these years that the forces that are to shape a biography are working at their deepest level. To that extent the little child is very much at the mercy of its adult environment both in what they offer of themselves and in what they assemble round it. It is underestimated how much this is the case, and the younger the infant the more is this the case. It is not sufficiently considered to what a degree the moral forces and the life processes are interrelated. A harsh, discordant, loveless or even sceptical environment that views the child as a young animal induces something like a slight freezing in the body-building process, a prelude to moral and physical weakness in later life, whereas a warm, gentle, loving and harmonious environment releases forces and quickens confidence and courage in life in the years to come. The former breeds antipathy, the latter fastens sympathy, and how much of our life is conditioned by the play of these two forces. It is an immense fallacy that little children do not notice. What they absorb unconsciously comes back as judgment when, in the course of the years, it rises up in consciousness. It would be wiser to think that nothing is missed, that everything is absorbed. Thus, too, premature intellectual methods of education, as described earlier, subdue life forces which will be needed for further development and promote a premature wakefulness which is misjudged as real progress, whereas it is really a foreshortening of life itself. It breeds precocity rather than genuine maturation which must always bide its own time.

The whole trend of today is towards over-intellectualization, furthered by the mass media misapplied. Do we not see the effects in our large scale social problems? It has been said that the child is father of the man; but we may add that it needs real children to make real men, and that to weaken the forces of childhood is to produce insecure adults. How else should whole populations succumb so easily to dictatorship or centralist rule in one form of another? Why should so many be ready to adopt state ruled moral codes for individual morality, state control for self-directed will? Yet these trends are everywhere. When the state begins to form men instead of men forming themselves, is not this evidence of impotence? How many are there today all the world over who feel they fall short of themselves in coping with the trials of life? But who will trace these conditions back to the years of earliest childhood? Hence it is that Rudolf Steiner so strongly advocated delaying reading and writing rather than hurrying them forward. Yet most parents get worried that their children are not learning fast enough.

A Waldorf Nursery class or kindergarten sets out to provide a right environment, right physical conditions, right activities, a right example for imitation.

The imitative faculty of the young child betokens an unconscious attitude of deep devotion to life; this, if unspoiled, finds beautiful expression in child play. If we were half as devoted and 'serious' in our adult activities as the child is in his play, we should be a different order of people. Child play finds its happiest and most intense experience in the natural imitation of all that grown-ups do, for, after all, the unconscious ideal of the child can only be to become a fully grown adult—everything in the child strives towards this. Nursery

Class education consist in 'doing' and in all doing it is the life of action
and of will that predominates. The objects of play should be as simple as possible to the end so that the child can clothe them with his
own natural powers of fantasy. A rough and ready doll made of a
piece of material or even out of a table napkin calls out these fantasy
forces, for to the little child everything is 'alive'; a 'perfect' doll may
seem to satisfy but in the end it cloys—it leaves no room for the
imagination and therefore works against the original and spontaneous
forces of childhood. These fantasy forces spring from a healthy life
of will like flowers from a meadow; they are crippled by 'clever'
toys invented by clever adults.

Who could wish for a happier sight than the following? We are
sitting in a nursery class, children aged about five. It is their hour
for free play.

Along comes a little boy. He has found a broom and is walking
along smartly, calling out, 'Sweep! Sweep!' As he comes by, his
glance is asking whether you have not a chimney for him to sweep.
You have only to indicate where it is. He recognizes it at once and
is all ready to serve. Have you ever seen such a sweep!

The children have recently had a puppet show. Some of them bring
you the wonders from behind the stage. They show you all the
characters and tell you who and what they are. They really *are*! Then
come others trailing after and carrying something very dangerous.
The look on their faces, the movements as they come, leave no room
for doubt. What can it be? The wicked wolf, of course, from Little
Red Riding Hood—not a make-believe thing as you might think with
its teeth and its red, red tongue. No, it is a wolf, every bit alive in
their imagination!

And now something else. Five or six children are busily setting
up something—just a few nursery chairs. What can it be? It is a coach!
Up goes the driver sitting in front and above. In come the passengers
sitting behind and below. And now, with a toot and a shout, away
they go. How intensely the driver scans the road lying ahead! How
full of purpose are the passengers looking out, silent, equally tense!
At what speed they are chasing through the countryside passing
everything by! And now they are drawing close! And now they have
actually arrived! Down comes the driver with a proud swagger. Out
jump the passengers. Who is there waiting to meet them? Ah, what

greetings, and what rejoicings, all talking copiously and together.

What an adventure! What more is needed? Is not this the great world itself? Play for the little child is not just pastime. What little child really *feels* little? Play is being grown-up. Play is work. Play is the world itself.

'Play' includes painting, modelling, cooking, sewing, building, making things and a host of entrancing activities; it also includes learning nursery rhymes and action songs in English, French and German, eurythmy (a new art of movement by Rudolf Steiner, not to be confused with eurhythmics), simple fairy tales, little plays, seasonal festivals—in fact, the Nursery Class or kindergarten is a world of its own, a world of dawning creation where life proceeds at its deepest level. The child should be left undisturbed in this world until nature herself declares the time ripe for change.

Waldorf Education teaches us to wait on Nature. Nature knows what she is about. Her signs are sure if only we can learn to read them. But we have grown far removed from nature. Instead of holding true to her we are ready to fall for any theory that is plausible, convenient and demands little from us. This is not a 'Back to Nature' call but only a plea that we become more wisely attentive to her. The change of teeth is a radical sign that the child is ready to enter upon a new stage.

'What then of the child who begins the change of teeth earlier— does that suggest earlier schooling?'

'No, it does not. On the contrary, such a child needs all the more protection from undue intellectual influence.'

'But what if a child is already reading, having picked it up willy-nilly without any help at all?'

'It is not good to negate a child, but you can regard the matter with a cool eye, and quietly engage the child in some interesting and colour-ful activities, engaging yourself in the process at times, then he will imitate you and be carried by your enthusiasm for this other.'

As for the child that is tardy with the change of teeth, it is generally advisable to wait. An analogy may be found with the process of birth itself: the child born prematurely needs added protection, care and warmth; on the other hand, the delayed birth causes no unusual concern unless, of course, it verges on the quite abnormal.

Chapter 3

THE CLASS-TEACHER YEARS
The Elementary School

The Elementary School covers the ages six to fourteen, thus forming the bridge from infancy to adolescence. Each new class, as it forms, receives a Class Teacher who stays with it for the whole eight years. (See the chapter that follows.) The founding school in Stuttgart was named The Free Waldorf School to signify that the teachers were to be free of outer authorities in building up the curriculum and in the treatment of subjects. It was also established that children would be entered into their classes according to chronological age.

How a teacher looks at life has a direct effect upon the children. It is basic to the character of a Waldorf School that a clear distinction is made between the nature of man and that of animal to a degree that is not yet customary in the world at large. It is then seen that such terms as infancy, childhood and adolescence leading on to a true adult state pertain only to the human being.

The following two examples drawn from the book *Man and Animal—their Essential Difference* by H. Poppelbaum will help to clarify this.

In the ape there are already some milk teeth at birth. The moment these are completed, which is within the first two years, second dentition begins. There is thus no room for infancy. In the human being the first milk teeth appear only several months after birth, and second dentition does not begin, normally, before the seventh year when the child has turned six. These are the years of infancy.

In the ape the sex glands are mature by the fifth year, and functioning begins immediately. In the human being, too, the sex glands are ready by the fifth year, but functioning is delayed by some ten years until puberty has set in. These are the years of childhood proper. But even so, body and the life of soul continue to grow and develop through the adolescent years, and, ideally, the inner life of soul should never stop growing.

It is seen that the animal hurries its physical development to an early end, and there it stops. Whereas, by contrast, the human being is subject to a law of restraint—he is held back physically, and thereby an education of soul is made possible leading into realms of inner realization and self-realization from which the animal is simply excluded.

There is no denying that the animal has a soul. It has desires and instincts and a range of emotions so far comparable to those of man that Darwin felt confirmed in his view that man and animal have a common origin, a view that today has become open to question. Instead of viewing man from the aspect of the animal, we may reverse the process and begin to perceive the animal from the aspect of man which is what Poppelbaum does in his book aforementioned. The following carries our considerations further.

Animal soul is bound to bodily functioning and set in a given physical environment. With domestic animals the same holds true except that human intervention may have modified the life habits and possibly the environment. With pets, dependence on man may have been carried so far as to become a vital factor for survival; they may pine and even die in the absence of master or mistress, exhibiting every sign of distress in the process. Nevertheless, the association still is in a strict sense 'bodily', concerned with usage and habits, and cannot be compared to the inwardness of human soul-relationships. Human soul experiences can arise through the very fact that in man alone the soul is partly emancipated from the body so that in him a self-sustained life of soul, an inwardizing of experience, becomes possible as the basis for *conscious personal experience.* And in so far as this emancipated life of soul can be objectified, can be freely contemplated and even modified at will, we recognize the penetration of the spirit. In this gradual emancipation and unfolding of an independent life of soul, in the gradual penetration of soul-awareness with ego-consciousness, we have the true meaning of childhood, the true passage from infancy through childhood to adolescence and adult life. In this lies the reason why nature is all-sufficient for the animal but only man can educate man. The animal grows into the outer kingdom of nature; the child needs also to grow into the inner kingdom of man.

The years from six or seven to fourteen are quite especially the unique gift of man. We make the gravest mistakes if we regard the child in these years merely as an incomplete version of the adult, and if we imagine that elementary education consists in simplifying adult knowledge, watering it down to a thin sort of gruel, sweetened with make-believe fairytales and other 'amusing' stories. This some people, and clever people at that, find hard to understand. It is easy to confound imagination with what is merely fanciful. It is equally easy to fall into the error of thinking that truth is only what is strictly rational. Cinderella is a work of imagination and we meet the truth it contains repeatedly in history and in life. Sinbad the Sailor is a clever invention to escape the tyranny of being eternally bound by what is rational. The former nourishes. The latter amuses. Both can serve if we know where they belong, but to know that, we need to discriminate between imagination and fanciful invention. The little child, still very close to his prenatal origin, brings into the world a deeply intuitive knowledge of what is true. Somewhere in his being he knows that truth is only truth if it brings revelation of the spiritual world from which he has come. It is this deep sense for truth which lived in the folk of long ago and which meets us today in folklore, in fairytales, in the great mythologies and sagas. The pictures these contain give nourishment to the people as a kind of heaven-born milk. The young child needs and longs for that kind of nourishment, not for what is merely fanciful nor for what is prosaically true, but for imaginative pictures which breathe of a higher reality. What is thus nourished through the picture will later grow into a faculty for virile, penetrating thought.

The picture we give the child must be a true picture, a picture born of truth. The picture speaks directly through the feelings to the heart; later the truth of it dawns for the mind. So often today the picture is merely for amusement, and truth is nothing but rationalism simplified for child consumption—no wonder that there is so much barren thinking in the world, thinking that time and again fails to cope with reality. The cause for this takes us back to the education, or rather mis-education of the little child. So much is spent today on 'higher education'. When will it be realized that the highest goal of education is with the little child? By the time he is grown up, it is mostly too late.

Truly we need to find the child in ourselves if we are to *know* children. We can impress our errors on them but we cannot evade the consequences—retribution comes in the form of fantasts who cannot find the ground under their feet or of fact-fanatics and iconoclasts who walk the earth staring into an empty universe. The greater danger today lies with the latter, a generation of men whose thinking is so far earthbound that they dismiss all forms of higher perception, including the arts, as unrealistic dreaming. Yet they would set up governments and rule the people. We have also seen signs of the opposite, a revolt against materialistic rationalism either through drugs or by diving back into various forms of oriental mysticism. The hope for the future lies in bringing new powers of imagination into our Western thinking so that human thought can once again testify to a world of higher realities which permeate our everyday living. To serve towards this end is perhaps the highest endeavour of Waldorf education—to lead through education towards the new enlightenment which all the best endeavours of our day, in art, in science, in religion are seeking. This places a great demand upon the teacher to pursue a disciplined way towards a higher grasp of human and natural existence. Unless we as adults can learn to reach up to our children as they descend towards us from worlds before birth, they, as they grow older, will find little or nothing to reach up to in us.

A teacher needs to be an artist, he needs to practise *the art of education*.

In teaching children between the ages of six and fourteen, our lessons will be different, both in content and method, from those given after puberty; the consciousness of the child in these years, the way things impress themselves upon him, the way life takes hold of him, are different; it is a preparatory time which conceals within itself what is to appear later. The flower is connected with its stem but it is not a stem; no more is adolescence, still less adult life, to be confused with that which lives in early childhood. The latter must be studied for itself—only then can we hope to prepare rightly for the next stage.

Careful observation will show, as already stated, that the change of teeth brings with it a subtle change of consciousness. The forces of soul which are now released appear as thought-forces, but they are not at all the intellectual thought-forces of the adult or even of the adolescent. For the analogy to this in human development as a whole we should have to go back to the myths and sagas of ancient times; their powerful pictures and imaginations, so penetrated with feeling, precede the age of thought. They are imbued with super-personal qualities belonging to the whole folk or community. The birth of intellectual thought is a recent event in world history; it dates back no further than the Greeks, the first philosophers, and even to them philosophy was anything but the abstract study it has since become. We need only note that the word they formed to describe their *new art of thinking*, philosophia, means *love of wisdom*—it comprises love and wisdom, the two greatest gifts and virtues of mankind. Even a book like Boethius' *Consolations of Philosophy*, which comes much later, shows us what deeply intimate and moral forces were involved; thought was like a sensitive seeing into spiritual depths of existence, more akin to poetry than to our present-day thought; it gave *inspired insight* into existence—that is how it was felt. Children of seven, if unspoiled by hasty methods and modern inventions like the cinema, TV and radio, think poetically, they think in imagery; their thinking is at the same time an art of feeling, a feeling-thinking born of the forces of the heart rather than of the head, a soul-thinking where revelation follows utterance as with the poet—it is not at all the analytical, critical head-thinking which comes, and of course should come, later. The years from seven to fourteen span an immense period of transition in the history of human experience. By fourteen the child stands much nearer to the threshold of the modern age, but even then his feeling life powerfully colours all his thinking, as indeed was still the case at the dawn of modern times in the fifteenth and sixteenth centuries—he has not yet reached in his development the purely speculative age, the age of self-detachment in thought.

All through these 'uncritical' years (that is to say, the years before the critical faculty of the intellect is freed), when judgment rests in feeling, touched but unpossessed by thought, the child longs for nothing more than for an authority he can trust with heart and soul. In these years the teacher stands before him, not only as a person, but as a representative of man; the child learns trust in humanity through his trust in a human being. In a Rudolf Steiner School this central position of trust is occupied by the class teacher.

What does this mean actually? It applies quite particularly to the main lesson period with which the day begins. (See description later).

It is here the class teacher's place is paramount. He meets his children day by day throughout his years with them, introduces all the main subjects for the year, English, History, Mathematics, the Sciences, and so on, and in the process learns to know his children intimately and to watch over their individual progress. After the main lesson, normally between 9 and 11 a.m. but in some countries earlier, his children are taken over by other teachers, specialists in language, music, eurythmy, handwork and other supporting subjects.

He, in turn, has his special subject to offer to children in other classes than his own, and thus connects up with other teachers and meets with children other than his own.

Thus every child meets several teachers and every teacher meets several classes. There is thus a close weaving and working amongst the teachers up and down the school. This provides for the utmost continuity as regards the children and for the greatest co-operation amongst the teachers, obviating any danger there might be towards onesidedness in the consideration of any given child.

The class teacher does more than teach subjects. He keeps close contact with the parents and with the school doctor if the school is fortunate enough to have one. He *cares* about his children, nurses qualities, guards against weaknesses, notes symptoms of poor health, strives to meet moral and mental difficulties; it is his business not only to instruct but *to bring up*, and he uses his subject matter and directs all his activities to the end of the *becoming man*. He steeps all he has to say in picture and imagination; life is a theme with many variations which follow one another in gradual descent from the ancient wonders of the spirit to the material and technological achievements of today. From year to year he takes up the main theme again, *the being of man*, in the course of years from fairytale and myth through ancient history down to our times, thus leading also via the prophets and the Christian mysteries to the promise of new fulfilments. The *picture* is the class teacher's medium, not the bare idea, for the former reaches down into the feeling life, the life of soul where all is contrast and movement, tension and relaxation, light and darkness, beauty and ugliness, joy and sorrow—contrasting experiences in epochs of history, in types of men, in plants and animals, in prose and poetry—an artistic and many-sided experience of the world and of man that is like a breathing within the soul, making

it rich and strong and well able to support the more conscious struggles
that are yet to come. Language teaching and recitation play an
important part in these years, handicrafts, wood carving, gardening
and especially painting, music and eurythmy—everything, in short,
that can further the life of rhythm in body and soul.

If *Nursery Class* education may be described as an education
through 'doing', that of the class teacher period from six to fourteen
becomes an education of the feelings and of the heart. We need a
generation of men and women with a stronger capacity for feeling,
for strong feeling born of rich soul experience—men and women with
greater heart; then, too, we shall have educated the social being of
man, for our heart is only our own to the extent that it beats for others.
The social element in man lives deeper than the intellect. One of our
main troubles today is that we have tried to intellectualize our social
problems instead of entering into them with imagination—and
imagination is a feeling force. The intellect divides us into our separate
selves but the heart, if rightly educated, reunites us again. Only the
heart can make the social bond. True community rests in the free
acknowledgment from man to man, so that the individual *grows* in
his response to his fellows; differentiation then becomes a moral good.
The only legitimate way to community is through understanding—
not by acceptance of a common theory, but by each individual learning
to transcend his personal viewpoint in the attempt to understand his
neighbour—that is the modern meaning of 'love thy neighbour as
thyself'. Until this is realized we shall not see peace. The education
we are describing sets out to try to overcome the primary evil, egotism.

As though in answer to his own question about 'the central thing',
the recording inspector, at the end of the second inspection referred
to earlier, earnestly pronounced the words, 'I think you are fighting
evil.' What he meant by 'evil' no one asked him. From conversations
with him before, during and after the inspection, I would dare to
suggest, as a possible interpretation, any influence that worked against
the uniquely moral, creative, and spiritually unbound nature of man.
It certainly is the greatest ideal of Waldorf education to work for the
full unfolding of the individual human spirit.

The social forces we are trying to foster in these schools are much
furthered by the fact that the community of the class during the eight
years with the class teacher remains unbroken. Since our concern is

for *all* the forces of childhood, the chronological age, not the mental age, is the determining factor for entry to a class. There are no marks, no obvious awards—there is help and counsel instead, and praise or correction as required. Instead of competition there is fostered the healthy spirit of emulation. Experience has shown that the latter is a far more potent stirrer of the will to achievement, the object no longer being success at all costs but sound results. The class, centred round the class teacher, is like a being of many members, each complementary to the rest; the achievement of the individual becomes the gift of the community.

There are countless opportunities for practising this. Time and again the teacher can draw attention to the happy use of an image, a phrase, even a word in the composition of this or that child, or a comparable instance in a painting, a drawing, the careful setting out of a page of arithmetic, and so on. There are slow heads and nimble fingers, clever heads and clumsy fingers, much room for mutual learning. We recall the instance of a child very gifted in art and handicrafts but exceptionally slow in arithmetic. She seemed quite incapable of grasping the nature of a fraction. She knew that one was one and that the number four was four, but why should one over four with a line between make a quarter? One morning, in front of the class, trying to understand the teacher, her eyes suddenly opened wide—she had seen it! And instantaneously the whole class burst into cheering. A moment of victory in which *all* participated. Such moments can become lifelong memories, now for one child, now for another.

The question may well be asked: What of the brilliant child, is he not likely to suffer by being held back? May he not feel thwarted and grow impatient and discontented? To this the counter-question may be put: What advantage is it to the brilliant child to be promoted, possibly even exploited and made a prize-show, on account of his brilliance? Brilliant he will be in any case but, divorced from a sufficient degree of humanity, will that be any real advantage to him or a source of true happiness? How many brilliant young people have been known to break down at some point either before or after entering college? How many people are there with brilliant minds who stand cut off from life with lamed wills? It is often just the brilliant child who needs our special care. Brilliance we need, but tempered with wisdom and compassion it is no longer merely brilliance. The mind of man, if it is to be robust and healthy, needs the heart to nourish it. A specialist on retarded children once explained to me her discovery that these children suffered from undernourishment of the brain. By means of diet and various exercises to improve circulation to the brain she achieved notable results. I essayed to explain our educational methods with younger children, how colour and imagination quicken sympathy, how sympathy works back on the breathing and the circulation, how our whole endeavour with the young who live essentially in their rhythmic system is to avoid abstract, bloodless thought, but instead to deepen feeling and strengthen the will—how in this way we were trying educationally to help all children and to nourish their senses and their nervous systems as she was trying medically to help her particular children. Out of her long experience she could only heartily agree.

We were taken by surprise when the school inspectors during their visit put the unexpected question: How is it that so few of your children wear glasses as compared with other schools? We could only attribute this to the same fact, that the teaching, by being imaginative and colourful, evokes greater interest and response, and that this works back healthily upon the whole body process even to the health of the sense organs. This explanation left the inspectors silent with wonder and apparently satisfied. A right education embraces the whole organism. Thought may be brilliant and yet brittle and emaciated. The hunger for knowledge is good if it is accompanied by a love for the good, the beautiful and the wise; this needs cultivating and it needs time. We need knowledge that is filled with life and minds that are alive in their thinking.

It is most important for the brilliant child particularly, whilst he is still a child, to learn the discipline of waiting for his fellows, helping where he can, and, more important, learning from his slower classmates who frequently have gifts and qualities of patience and perserverance which he may lack. But a Rudolf Steiner education is many-sided, appealing to *all* the faculties and with the younger child especially it is the *all* that matters far more than exceptional proficiency in one respect. We want rounded, complete and balanced personalities whose special gifts are nourished from a fuller source. The community of the class with its central guide, maintained with all the human differences it comprises through the eight most formative years of school life, provides for this. A deeper, richer life of heart is needed to humanize the intellect. If the teacher is wise and if the teaching is wise, the brilliant child need never be at a loss. There is an abundance of activity to engage him and ample scope to satisfy his needs. Let him add body and character to his brilliance and he will be a better and more full-blooded specialist when his time comes.

There is, however, a broader consideration. Rudolf Steiner discriminates between wakeful children, dreaming children, and children who are relatively in a kind of slumber. For the years we are considering, life at its best should be a happy childhood dream. The transition from the pure fantasy of the little child to the abstract thought of later years should be a gentle process. The wakeful or over-wakeful child needs to be quietened and harmonized by engaging him in every possible form of artistic and practical activity, by presenting him with every possible example of true endeavour, by winning from him qualities of reverence and respect, calling upon him to acknowledge what has shown itself as noblest, greatest and best in others—by teaching him the hard and patient way. The slumbering child also needs careful watching—he may even *appear* to be retarded. Here the method is not to attack the head, which merely produces headaches, but to train the will through action and repetition. Let him learn little, to begin with, but let him learn it thoroughly, from the crown of his head to the toes of his feet. If it is a case of memorizing something, for example, let him go back and forth on the classroom floor, if only for a few minutes each day, clapping and stamping between each word of the line to be remembered; so, too, with his other learning work. Just as we feel best after a deep sleep, so these 'deep sleepers' may have most to give when, eventually, they do awaken; they may be slumbering men of genius who, just because they have so much to express later, need longest to mature. Or their slumber may be an assumed mode of self-protection from this noisy, clamorous world so that the soul may grow in peace. Such children may be won by good-humoured patience and encouragement.

In short, the class as a small community of varying elements prepares for the great community of life. It is a special privilege to be allowed to grow up in this way and to learn from the earliest years 'to bear with one another'—for what is the meaning of compassion but to bear with, to suffer with?

From the teacher's point of view, the passage through the eight years leaves little room for hackneyed routine; he has constantly to be astir. His work is hard, but it becomes his life and his recreation for he re-creates himself through it. The children that leave him are his friends for life and so are their parents.

An understandable question: What if a child should not like his class teacher—is it not protracted misery and torture to have to put up with him for so long? In my experience no such case has ever arisen (but see the next chapter). The answer is not far to seek. From the description given in these pages, it will be seen that this education has as its heart and core the striving to understand man at his deepest level; this lifts the thoughts and feelings above the personal and sub-jective. The question is always what the child needs and what will best meet those needs for his total development. Where the experience of the single teacher fails, he has the collective experience of all his colleagues whom he meets weekly for this purpose. There is thus no room left for petty likes and dislikes, and if the teacher does not have them it is rare for the children to have them. For the most part parents are amazed at the love and trust of their child in his or her class teacher. Indeed, the gratitude of parents on behalf of their children has been one of the mainstays of our work, and the main cause of its growth.

A very important aspect of the work in a Rudolf Steiner school is the consideration given not only to the 'how' but to the 'when'. Illuminating articles will be found in *Child and Man*, a joint publica-tion of the Waldorf Schools in Great Britain, the United States and Canada. It is our view that the child, evolving *in time*, recapitulates not only the biological laws of the human race, but, in mood, feeling and mode of perception re-lives the entire history of man; therefore the time for introducing a given subject must be considered as well as the manner of doing so.

Parents of young children are confronted with the fact that reading is delayed in our schools—that we follow the slow procedure of going from movement and gesture to painting, drawing and writing, only finally leading over to actual reading. In this we pursue the normal path set out by history. If the teacher of the child of six has taken the trouble to engage his imagination with a story; if then, out of the story he selects a picture, say of a wave, and then the child runs waves, paints and draws waves and eventually comes to a flowing ⌣⌣ and finally to the crystallized hieroglyphic W, he has been led along the way of experience to a conclusion; he has not been forced to a conclusion. The child grows connected in limb and heart and eye with this conclusion; it has become *his* conclusion. This takes longer but it brings inestimable benefit. It is so easy to teach the child the letter directly; he then has to accept it as a symbol foreign to himself, a dogma coming at him from outside, and he will do so; the result, however, is that deep below consciousness, in feeling and in will, the sense of having been impressed upon, the *sense of dogma* lives on and later may appear as a constraint of the mind—a feeling of estrangement from a world which merely confronts him and which he may never hope to penetrate. Writing, which for the Egyptians was still a sacred heavenly script, has become for us a mere convention. To the child taught in the way described, knowledge is something born of a world of imagination, a world of experience beyond the senses and the physical facts and yet accessible—he cannot yet translate this into thoughts, but in the years to come his attitude to life will surely show it. Having been *led* on his descent to where he finds himself, he is not likely to feel himself so much a stranger on this earth, and may eventually discover in himself the will and the courage to advance from the known to the unknown, from the 'letters' which he perceives spread out all around him to the spirit. If there was a real way down there must also be a real way up! By guiding the child in accordance with a real past, placing each exercise at the right time, we open for him the possibility of a way into a real future. To many, especially at first sight, this may seem laboured, but others will find it sound psychology. And those who have had the privilege of following such children right through even to the age of eighteen, and have held converse with them at different periods during that time, and have then watched them proceeding into life, will know how much truth lives in such matters, and how such apparently slight beginnings hang with the weightiest results. The 'how' is here the transition from the picture to the letter; the 'when', the time when the child's natural phantasy *begins to turn earthwards*.

A further example. It is a Goethean principle, which science is coming close to rediscovering and which Rudolf Steiner often emphasized, that the whole is reflected in each of its parts. Thus the whole development up to twenty-one is reflected in each of the three subdivisions, from birth to the age of seven, from seven to fourteen and from then to the event of coming-of-age. With regard to the middle of these three periods, there is a carrying over of the imitative stage up to about the age of nine; there then follows what my colleague, A.C. Harwood, in his book *The Way of a Child*[1] most happily calls 'the heart of childhood', from about ten to twelve; and finally, from twelve to fourteen, a period which anticipates in many ways the birth of adolescence.

Now the age of nine to ten is a particularly sensitive one in a child's life, marked by a variety of symptoms. It really corresponds to that moment in the first period of life at about the age of three when the child first says 'I' to himself and memory begins. Whereas that first flash of ego-consciousness is a purely intuitive one, now there is a gentle deepening of self-perception in the life of feeling. It is the first dawning of the realization of being 'alone' and separate in the world. With some this accentuation of self may take an assertive, even an aggressive form; with others it may show itself as a feeling of insecurity, of wanting to cling to others—there may even be night-fears, so well described by Lamb; also the children become more attentive to their surroundings, to the habits and mannerisms of their teachers and parents, for example, who are now seen to be capable of *making mistakes*; sometimes—mostly where there has been a lack of loving understanding on the part of the adults—there are distressing episodes of stealing, as though the child is trying to compensate for a 'sense of loss' by taking and appropriating things. To meet this moment in child experience Rudolf Steiner made a number of suggestions which serve to illustrate how concrete this education strives to be.

For the story-telling material he called attention to the Old Testament. Beginning with the separation of Adam from his God, we follow, through Noah, Moses, the Patriarchs, and so on, the progressive descent of man into earthly existence. Story after story describes how the individual stands in life to realize and to serve that which is greater than himself—that which is 'of God' in him. The sense of 'self' in man finds supports in a 'sense of origin' and a 'sense of mission'. Experience has proved time and again what strength, comfort and encouragement flows to the nine-year-old from this source,

1. A.C. Harwood. *The Way of a Child*, Rudolf Steiner Press, London, 1988.

how his enthusiasms are engaged, his fears allayed. I, too, have a destiny.

As a companion subject the children are taught about farming, about the farmer—and of course the farmer's wife! The farm is a community of life; it includes the creatures, the plants, the soil itself; it relates to the great cycle of the seasons and leads the gaze from earth to heaven and back again; it comprises so many 'human activities', in the field, in the barn, in the home, at the mill—so many forms of service in which man is seen at his best, as the simple servant and representative of God—the master who serves for the good of all; it reveals man as a being who is *more* than nature and yet who stands fully within nature; one who can *order* life for mutual benefit and blessing—a husband-man.

It was at the end of such a period, in recapitulating the work covered, that a teacher asked his class, 'What then is needed if the farmer is to expect a good harvest?' The children thought of everything they could: sun and moon and rain and wind and weather, the farmer (and the farmer's wife to keep him up to it, piped up a girl to a chorus of approval from the other girls) and the farm hands, and the farm equipment, of course, and so on. 'Still not enough,' said the teacher. There was a lengthy pause and then a shy, usually reticent boy at the back of the class put his hand up, 'The droppings of the animals!' The children laughed. How stupid not to have thought of this before! It needed very few words on the part of the teacher to evoke a mood of wonder, even of awe, at this simple, everyday phenomenon. Such is the great household of nature, where each thing has its place, where all things serve, where nothing is ever lost, nothing wasted.

The children were too young for the teacher to comment on the lamentable rôle which man has come to play in this connection—that was to be reserved till they were older.

At another time in the same year the children are taught about house-building and all the detailed skills involved, and how the house, in all its parts, is an extension of man himself with his daily human and social needs: the dining room for eating, the kitchen for preparing foods, the bathroom, the lavatory, the library for study, the sitting room for entertaining, the bedroom for sleep and relaxation, and so on.

Or to touch on quite a different theme, the approach to grammar and syntax. Already in the second class the children will have been introduced to 'doing' words, 'describing' words, and 'naming' words. Now this can be carried further to the structure of a sentence. Every sentence must have a subject and a predicate which tells us what the subject is doing or where he is. Let the reader join in the exercise with the eight to nine year olds. Let him ask himself, for example, what a stone can do, what a plant can do, what an animal can do, or this or that particular animal, and finally what a man can do. Let him experience the immense, the almost unlimited expansion of possibilities when it comes to man. Then let him imagine what this can mean to a young child, how simply through the exercise the child comes to realize, in his feelings to begin with, but later in his understanding, how man represents a totally new dimension of being, one that ranges far beyond his physical needs and limitations, so that he can never be identified with the animal as is the common practice in our times. Once again, so much depends on when a particular exercise is introduced, at what *time* in a child's life according to the inner needs and conditions of the child at that time. The exercise in question suits so admirably the first delicate moment of self-awareness. Somewhere from the depths of his being there is an answering echo, as yet unexpressed, 'I know what *man* is'.

It is observation of the child which must be our guide ever and again. The approach to the twelfth year of life brings new changes which must be carefully prepared for, changes which are precursors of puberty. Development varies, with some manifesting earlier, with others later, yet all children at this time begin to grow a little *out of rhythm*; this can be seen very well, for example, in their gymnastics, where their movements tend to become less gracious and carefree and demand more thought and deliberation. As the children become more aware of their bodies they also experience weight and gravity differently—the mechanics of the bones come into play, however gently at first. Only now are they ready to study the mineral world, the kingdom of the lifeless, and to have their first introduction to the science of physics. In the third class (American third grade) they had man as man, in the fourth class man and the animals, in the fifth class man and the plants, and now at the age of twelve, in the sixth class, man and the stones, and also physics: the eye in relation to colour, to light and darkness, to shadows and elementary perspective; the ear in relation to sound, to noise and tone, the intervals, the mathematics of the monochord; the whole body as sense organ for warmth and cold; the meaning of expansion and contraction, within the soul and outside in nature; also a first acquaintance with the mysterious world of the depths, with magnetism and electricity. Details of this must be sought in the articles to which reference has been made. Here it is the time element we wish to stress. Time is not just a chronological affair—that is time reduced to dead mechanics. In the *process* of time, real things happen; in the time process of child development the most vital things happen. Time here means life, and the teacher must be alive enough to know the right thing to do at the right time. To work 'out of time' is to invite disharmony, but to interpret time in the right way needs the kind of insight into human nature which Rudolf Steiner has given.

At about this time, too, children begin to 'shoot' into their limbs, and eventually comes that awkwardness of limb which is the bane and confusion of the young adolescent. To meet this they are introduced, from about the age of twelve, to wood-carving, demanding as it does quite special and controlled use of the limbs; they learn the use of tools, and how to overcome the resistance of a hard material which has to be shaped exactly according to intention; they learn also to experience the plastic possibilites inherent in the human hand itself. At the same age, where possible, they begin to have regular gardening lessons, again the learning of the use of tools, and the handling, this time, of the soil itself. The whole of our social and economic life rests on the soil. What better introduction to becoming a true man on earth than to learn to know the soil in the round of the seasons—but the time to begin this must be read from the child.

In history they learn about the people who made themselves conquerors of the earth; about the Romans who, out of their consolidated strength, sent out their legionaires north, south, east and west, upon the solid highways which they themselves constructed; but also about those same Romans who established civil law and citizen rights and first made room for the *individual* in society. What more solid piece of flesh can be imagined than that of the Roman in his might? And what strength and what assurance of oneself *within the body* does this not bring to the twelve-year-old! The body is the temple of the spirit. The children must make a healthy entry into their bodies—that is their direct way if they are eventually to find the spirit. Always the balance must be maintained. If then the children go on to learn of Arabic culture with its speculative thought and abstract Algebra, learning at the same time of the Crusaders and their battles for the earthly city of Jerusalem, they also hear of Arthurian knighthood, and of the Knights of the Holy Grail, fighters for the heavenly kingdom, 'the holy city set on a hill'.

These few examples from the practical teaching will have to suffice for the purposes of this small introductory book. Before, however, we leave the class teacher in his work and the childhood years which are his special concern, we need to reflect somewhat further on what his full rôle is, and why, if his work is to be fully effective, he needs to accompany his children for the full life span from the close of infancy to entry into adolescence.

It is the business of any teacher to impart knowledge in the best way he can and to attend to the disciplines connected with learning. If he is truly a teacher he will most certainly feel a deep concern for his children and he will enjoy helping them surmount difficulties both in the work and socially as these arise. Yet in most cases today he has them at a given age and only for one year. He has little or no knowledge of what went before and what is to come after. A class teacher, however, has a whole irreplaceable life span of eight years. Through the subjects he teaches he learns to know his children ever more intimately as they progress through the years. His business is to prepare them for a healthy entry into life. By the time they leave him he will have introduced them to the kingdoms of nature, to the stars above and the earth below. Through his history they will come to understand that life is least of all a haphazard affair, but that there are great interventions, there is meaning and destiny. The study of individual biographies helps greatly towards this. His geography lessons will go to demonstrate the interdependence of human beings, more in our present age than ever before, and how economic life, and the basis of mutual service it entails, calls for brotherhood amongst men. It is such threads he has to draw together into pictures and imaginations that can reach the feelings and fire the will, preparing for the years to come when they will have to find the guide and teacher in themselves. For much that he teaches the fuller understanding will dawn later, perhaps many years later when, confronting a particular problem or situation, there will flash through the mind the meaning of something said long ago and long forgotten. Such a flash of recognition rising up from childhood memories brings an added joy to life and often new courage to proceed. These are the further goals of the class teacher, indeed of any real teacher, but the class teacher has immensely greater possibilities.

In his daily practice, however, the class teacher also has his more intimate tasks. He is not only a friend and guide. He needs in many respects to be also a therapist. The following, by way of illustration, is near enough to the facts to be taken as a case history.

Evelina came up into the first class (or grade) from the nursery school. She was tall for her age, pale, with a slight drag in her movements as though her body was too heavy for her, and very sensitive in her feelings, over-sensitive in regard to those around her. Her eyes had a questioning look even at that young age. She could smile but rarely laughed outright. She tended to draw back into herself and *felt* left out even when she was not. She could not enter easily into play with others and this made her both sad and resentful. On the other hand she painted beautifully and had a most delicate and lovely sense of colour. Alone with the sheet of paper in front of her and the paints or crayons beside her she could be totally absorbed and happy. Her paintings were always admired by her classmates. They were generous in their praise. This was her closest social medium but it still left her lonely.

Her persistent sense of loneliness, largely self-imposed, led to a curious development. By no means an intellectual child, she was nevertheless way ahead of the other children in learning to read. She became a voracious reader but remained one of the worst spellers. Reading was her way of escape from the world around her. She skimmed the words in her eagerness to get lost in the story, but had no time to *look* at the words and see how they were composed. The more she read, the lonelier she grew, and the lonelier she grew the sadder she became. She came to feel she was a kind of outcast and she wanted to hide away.

The class teacher arrived one morning with a story about a seed. The seed had been blown by the wind from far away. It fell into a deep crevice, cut off from everything around it. It was dark and damp down there and terribly lonesome. The seed was most unhappy and lay there sorrowful and without hope. There was a brief moment in the day, however, which was different from all the rest. During that short while the crevice where it lay was suddenly filled with light and even with warmth. It was the moment when the sun high in the heavens passed by overhead. It was then and then only that something seemed to stir in the seed. Was it a dream of long ago or a vision of some distant time to come? At any rate, now the seed waited and waited each day for that moment to come. It lived for that moment and when it came it reached up as high as it could towards the sun. The seed was no longer a seed but a tiny plantling and, hardly noticing it, it grew just a little bit taller each day. At length came the day when it had grown tall enough to see the world around—to see and to be seen. What wonder that vision brought to our plantling, but the greatest wonder was the surprised and happy greeting of the flowers around. What a greeting they gave the stranger. the like of which they had never seen before!

The story made a strong impression on the class but particularly on Evelina. Neither she nor anyone else suspected why that story had been brought to them. The story was retold by different children on successive mornings. It gave rise to class conversations, to crayoning and to painting, and certainly made a difference. One such story is not enough. Some little time later it was followed by another story, but the emphasis now was upon the attitude of the class. There was once a queen who rejoiced much in the flower gardens around her palace. The time was early spring and there was one bed in particular, a tulip bed, cared for by none other than the head gardener. You know how a tulip grows out of a bulb. As the sun grew stronger, the tulip bulbs began to grow eager and impatient to send up their beautiful tall stems and leaves. And now, as the bulb below grew less bulbous, up above there were forming the tulip buds, and presently the flowers began to appear in all their brilliant colours. The tulips were a gay company as they grew in rings of colours in their circular flower bed. There was one tulip at the very centre which seemed to be the slowest, as if it was hiding something specially precious. All the other tulips were waiting and watching for it to open and wondering whatever that tulip would really look like. There were red tulips and yellow tulips of many different shades. Whatever would this tulip be? Well, one day, the bud began to open, and what should be there but something very dark, not a very dark red or a very dark blue, but something black. This shocked all the other tulips. A black tulip was something quite monstrous. They felt ashamed, humiliated in fact. They felt that the black tulip ruined their whole flower bed. They wondered whatever the queen would think when she came along, and they wondered why the head gardener did not take this tulip out right away but instead came every day to look at them all but looked longest of all at the black tulip, shining with its own dark mystery. Well, the day came when the queen and the head gardener were coming straight towards them. They trembled at the thought of the queen's displeasure at this black in their midst. As the queen came closer, they tossed their heads indignantly to show that they well knew the disgrace the head gardener had placed upon them. There was quite a chatter amongst them, a special kind of tulip chatter. And then they grew deadly still and silent.

The queen came right up to their tulip bed and said, 'Oh, gardener, what wonderful tulips you have growing there, the loveliest tulips in the whole of my kingdom. How tall they are, what colours they possess, in reds and yellows and golds and royal purples.' Then the queen's eyes fell on the tulip in the middle. All the tulips shivered, wondering what dreadful thing would happen now. Whoever had heard of a black tulip! The queen bent down to see more clearly and her eyes opened wide. 'Oh, gardener, what have we here? This is the greatest wonder of them all. You must please bring it into the palace for the King to see.' The other tulips were taken completely by surprise. They craned forward to have a really good look before it was taken away. They had never really looked before. And now, as the sun shone brightly down on them, they saw the deepest, deepest possible purple glinting through the festive black. A great silence fell upon them. When that tulip was gone, a sadness descended on them all—they all felt lonelier and could not help feeling ashamed as they looked at one another, ashamed not of the tulip which had gone but of one another.

Again, the children had no notion at all why this story had been told them. Added to the previous story, it had a decisive effect. The world is full of story, but to create a story to meet a given situation comes as a quite special gift and brings its own reward. Such timely remedial stories belong very much to the tasks of the class teacher. It has been said that almost every class has a Cinderella in it and that children can be cruel. Closer observation has shown that when there is a child suffering from a deep insufficiency of one kind or another it tends to draw on the other children and to sap their energies, and this calls forth an inevitable resistance in self-protection. This needs to be remedied for the sake of all.

In her third school year, Evelina gave striking evidence of such an insufficiency. That is the year for the Bible stories as described previously. It can well be imagined that the story of Joseph would appeal to her particularly, he the dreamer with the coat of many colours, who was different from his brothers, who was specially loved by his father and therefore all the more hated by them so that they cast him out and sold him into slavery. But he was destined to become a mighty overlord, a dispenser of bread. The time came when these same faithless brothers knelt before him, not daring to look up at him. And then they heard him say, 'I am Joseph, your brother whom ye sold into Egypt.' Then they were grieved and were full of fear, but he called them 'brothers' and opened his arms to them.

Thus, in the course of the work, one opportunity followed another, bringing healing with it, and then the source of Evelina's difficulties revealed itself in an unusual fashion. When she was about nine she began to draw, paint, model witches, flying or sitting, with or without a broomstick—with their black cloaks and tall hats and great humps on their backs. The teacher was amazed and so were the children, so was Evelina herself in a kind of way. She had no explanation for it. It just happened again and again with no connection whatsoever with the work of the class. The witch had become her obsession. Children have a genius for projecting out of themselves something troubling them inwardly. What was Evelina trying to cast off? The teacher turned to the doctor and the doctor discovered that the child was exceptionally hollow-chested. Her round-shouldered appearance which gave the impression of her wishing to shut herself off had a visible cause. The ever-recurring hump was a compensatory image for the hollow which was actually there. The doctor helped, the curative eurythmist helped (see section on eurythmy), the kitchen helped, so did the art work in colour (the out-going red rather than the receding blue), and modelling (the convex rather than the con-cave form), the Old Testament stories with their tales of courage and endurance in the face of difficult trials and circumstances; every teacher helped in every way he could to fill that hollow space. Evelina grew more balanced in health, in her general demeanour and social bearing, more harmonious and more confident. She was getting rid of her hump. Still a melancholic, from being caught up in sorrow for herself her warm imaginative nature learned to stream out more readily in sympathy for the needs of others. She became much loved in the class.

At the age of twelve something further occurred which was quite unpredictable. This child who loved reading so much was forbidden all access to books, even to the strain of writing things down, for she was threatened with blindness. The patience and the quiet courage with which she faced this ordeal won the further love and admiration of all around her. In the end, with careful treatment, this danger was averted. In later life Evelina became a strong and generous character, a successful artist, and a happy wife and mother.

This narrative is offered as an example—every class teacher will have similar narratives—to show how the timely understanding of a teacher can intervene deeply in the life and destiny of the children in his care, and why it is so important to maintain the continuity of relationship throughout the formative years of childhood. Not only in the methods of teaching, but almost more so in the handling of daily life, do we see the true meaning of authority, authority in the service of the freedom to come.

When the class teacher first sets out on his journey, the eight years stretch like an eternity ahead, but looking back one wonders where they have gone. There are class teachers who have gone through the eight year period three times, four times, in rare instances even five times. 'Do not think repeating the process means that you will do it better the next time,' says Rudolf Steiner. It will not necessarily be better, it will be different: different children, changing circumstances, a new stage in the teacher's own life—indeed, there is no such thing as repetition, only ever-new creation. We can never merely repeat a life experience.

The years between twelve and fourteen are the most subtly difficult to manage. As the children approach puberty, the intellectual faculty begins to make greater demands, with some children more than with others. There are, in every class, children who are eager, almost too eager, to move on, and other who would wish to cling longer to their childhood. Whilst providing new exercises for the thinking, the imaginative treatment of subjects should not too readily be relinquished. There is always the danger of confusing the pre-adolescent symptoms with actual adolescence. 'Truth' even at fourteen rests more in the vivid *experience* of single events, in the noble sympathies and antipathies of given characters, than in comprehensive ideas and sequences; the children are still immersed in the living content of things; the detached and more or less objective survey comes later.

Chapter 4

THE EIGHT-YEAR CLASS TEACHER
A Clarification

On first hearing that in a Waldorf School a teacher carries a class right through the elementary school years from age 6 to 14, the question naturally arises, 'What if the child doesn't get on with the teacher? Would that not be a fearful imposition?' The fact is that such a case occurs extremely rarely, and that needs explanation.

It must be clear that the class teacher is normally with his class during main lesson time only, that is for the first two hours of the morning. After that time other teachers take his children in the non-main lesson subjects, languages, music, eurythmy, hand crafts, gymnastics, games and so on, whilst during that time he teaches in other classes. That means that every class teacher must have a special subject of this kind.

This arrangement means that the children are by no means confined to one teacher, that the class teacher has this group of colleagues round for consultation at any time, and that he serves similarly in other classes in association with other class teachers. Each class teacher is certainly a central figure for his children and their parents, but the teachers together create a *web* of interrelated gifts and faculties. The class teacher, by teaching in other classes than his own, enters more widely into the life of the school.

The picture of a Waldorf School is thus one of the daily interweaving of human beings with their different abilities and fields of responsibility, all united in the goals they serve, which are to lead every child that comes to them along a path towards greater fulfilment in life. The teacher himself is always engaged in a learning process to further his work. The whole nature of the work carries it beyond the merely personal and protects it from onesidedness. A child is known to several teachers, and, if a problem arises, the class teacher has the benefit of their several observations and suggestions. If need be, the matter is brought before the whole College of Teachers for even wider consideration.

In these circumstances, as already stated, an impasse between a child and the class teacher occurs only very rarely. If it does, it has to be studied thoroughly and a solution found. There have been instances where a lack of confidence in the teacher by the parents has led to such an impasse. In that case, rather than live in this lack of accord between home and school, it is best for the child to leave. There have also been rare instances where it has seemed best to move a child into an adjacent class; every class has a range of a year within it and there have been borderline cases where the actual connection with the other group of children as well as with their class teacher has proved beneficial. Experience has taught that a wonderful bond of loving respect grows up between the children in a class and their class teacher which carries forward far into life.

In regard to this question of continuity there are other important considerations. It may be asked: 'How long does it take an experienced teacher to know thirty children or more—really to *know* them, understand them and be able to enter into their intimate needs?' And the contrary, 'How long does it take children to grow so accustomed to the quality of mind, the temperament, the mannerisms of a teacher that they feel happily anchored, understood and secure?' And what can it mean in a child's life to have to make a new adjustment to a personality every year again? What can be the effect on a young child of being thus uprooted and transplanted year by year during the most formative years of its life—a different quality of discipline as well as all else?

And what does it mean to a teacher to be for ever dealing with the same age group, the six year olds, the nine year olds, and so on, knowing hardly at all what went before and without responsibility for what comes after? Where is the sanity in this which is accepted as the universal practice?

We have seen that a child's life is not only a succession of years— it is a life-developing process, and like all such processes there are nodal points and intervals and crises, that is, times of vital transition which have to be specially known, prepared for, met and carried over. All this is part of a teacher's profoundest service, and how can it be achieved without the kind of continuity with the children in their growing, and with their parents? How, in these turbulent times, can we hope to find people with inner strength of security, feeling strongly anchored in themselves and in their tasks in life, if they have not experienced that anchorage and security in their growing years? All these are questions to be faced. The benefit and the wisdom of Waldorf practice have found their proof in the lives of many thousands of adults who look back with deep gratitude to their years with their class teacher.

Another question arises, 'Where do you find teachers of the calibre to undertake such an eight-year programme?' They are not found all at once. They have to be continually finding themselves, learning, growing, advancing from stage to stage with the help of others in their own school or in other schools who have gone before. There is no repetition of last year—every year is a new adventure, a continuous exploration, not easy, but in its effect a life-renewing process; a life of growing and becoming, maturing and discovering, in intimate working with one's colleagues—a life of dedicated service to the child becoming man.

At the end of the eight years what happens to the teacher then? He or she should have a sabbatical. Rudolf Steiner's advice was to engage during that year in a quite different type of activity, to travel, to make new connections. Then, if they come back to take a second class through, will that be easier? Maybe in some ways, but it will never be the same; it is not just a case of different children, but children have become different, and the teacher is different, is older and working out of other forces, and life, too, has become different. It will be a new adventure all over again.

Chapter 5

ABOUT TEMPERAMENTS

A striking innovation on the part of Rudolf Steiner in the sphere of education, but also in life in general, is his introduction of the study of the four temperaments. In the days of Shakespeare and Ben Jonson these were spoken of as the 'humors' or 'humours', related to the word 'humid', moist. They were based on what were regarded as the vital fluids:

> blood—sanguine (a sanguine temperament);
> black bile—choleric (easily galled, angered, irritated);
> yellow bile—melancholic (liverish, peevish, jaundiced);
> and phlegm—as the word suggests, phlegmatic, sluggish.

Once we begin to pay attention to them, the temperaments convey much for daily observation. We all must be related to all four, since we all possess the four vital fluids, yet it is striking to note how each one has a dominant temperament and must take care not to be at the mercy of it. Let us say we all, at times, have a choleric burst of temper—the moment passes but the habitual temperament remains: the choleric is apt to be the most stormy, and later the first one to regret it; the sanguine, feeling he has been caught out, will try to pass things off with a laugh; the melancholic is likely to brood longest and remain in sombre mood; the phlegmatic may be quite startled with himself, then shrug his shoulders and quietly move on.

The temperaments have their virtues and their vices. The choleric is a courageous fellow, the first to mount the battlements, but he can also be foolhardy and unrestrained in his ire. The sanguine is generally a good mixer, a good one to have in any company, but he can be easily forgetful, inconsequent and therefore not wholly reliable. The melancholic is thoughtful by nature and ready to reach out to others in their distress—but he can be too busy dabbing his own eyes and is then a general wet blanket. The phlegmatic can at times present himself as a solid rampart of defence if he is not, on the contrary, slowing up all the traffic in the highway. The ideal of anyone is to achieve mastery of his temperament, but that means reaching a source in oneself which carries beyond the play of temperament so that one learns to live equably with all around.

We now turn to the question of how this relates to the education of children. How far is it possible to help children develop the virtues of their temperaments, avert or overcome their vices, and so grow towards becoming 'masters of all weathers' both in public and in private life? We offer the following small-scale incident by way of illustration.

There was once a summer camp in the west of England for children from the Michael Hall School. Quite a contingent, on this occasion, came over from the Waldorf school in Stuttgart to join them so that, together with two or three teachers and other helpers, we were a company of around seventy.

We started off in very good cheer, but then the weather turned out to be relentlessly foul. If it didn't blow it rained and often both at once and that almost incessantly—quite the worst it could be. We cooked over a trench fire mostly in rain. We huddled together in the main tent at meal times and for a social hour in draught and in damp. One early morning saw half of the campers struggling out of the tents that had collapsed on them as a result of the wind and on to the sodden ground outside. Another morning at 4 a.m. a brave young crew set out with frying pans and sausages and other delicate viands to march to a distant hill from which to view the rising sun and feast in its honour. They reached the hill top well on time, but then came the clouds, and never a glint of sun; having waited hopefully for a time, they took to frying their sausages while the rain sizzled on to the frying pans, ate hurriedly and beat a hasty retreat, if not for 'home', then at least for home base. Then, half way back, the sun decided to come out in radiant smiles, a poor consolation but not to be despised; and so they arrived in camp, not beating drums or even frying pans, but carrying their heads high— for, after all, they *had* got up at 4 a.m., and what had the others done? Indeed, there *were* bursts of sunshine from time to time, which meant a rush to air the tents and get things dried out.

Yet, with it all, so strong was the resolve, by common consent, and at all costs, 'to brave the weather', that no more than one or two in the whole camp succumbed to a catarrh. The cholerics, true to type, blew their chests in defiance of those dismal weather-gods; the sanguines rollicked with good humoured laughter; the melancholics, looking around and seeing there was no help for it, dried their eyes, buried their handkerchiefs and grew unusually cheerful; and the phlegmatics allowed themselves to be rolled out of their security coverings to do their share of the chores, and whatever else, with unremitting grace. All were happy with all and took pride in all. It was declared in the end with hearty bravado and three loud cheers that this was the best camp that ever was—no one dared to suggest that ever could be. The camp was able to throw a concert to the village in the village hall: music, songs and scenes from *A Midsummer Night's Dream*, with the local M.P. as the guest of honour. He, seeing the British and the Germans so heartily united, made a redoubtable speech about how such a camp showed the way towards universal harmony and peace.

What is the point of this story? We certainly had mastered the circumstances by appealing to something more than temperaments, yet whereby each temperament could play its role. In life, too, there are all kinds of inclement weathers. Another of Shakespeare's comedies ends with the Clown, left alone on the stage when all the rest of the company have gone, singing a song, a sad and lonesome song, with the refrain 'For the rain it raineth every day.' Why should it rest with the Clown, dressed in Fool's motley, to be the one to see most clearly the foolishness, the Folly of this world? And every young person must go through such a moment of loneliness, of wondering at the folly of the world—far greater folly today than in Shakespeare's time, and then how many take their guise from their temperaments, the rebellious choleric, the careless sanguine, the repining melancholic, the indifferent phlegmatic.

Once entered upon seriously, the work with the temperaments, as introduced by Rudolf Steiner, opens up real possibilities of helping children towards coming level with themselves and therefore with the world. It offers opportunities in a great variety of ways, for example in the approach to the four rules in arithmetic, to the choice of a personal instrument in music, to exercise in colour, in drawing, to

the distribution of parts in a play preferably written by the teacher
for his class, to the tasks he might set for one child or another both
in their school work and their services to the class; they also relate
to matters of discipline, of health, even of diet, in consultation with
the parents.

Rudolf Steiner recommended that children should be grouped in
class according to their temperaments. This way the teacher has a
clearer command of the whole situation of the class. His golden rule is
never to go *against* the temperament of a child but always to go *with* it.
In telling a story, or narrating a piece of history, he has this well in
mind. For example, should he be describing a monarch, a captain, a
situation depending on someone's daring or courage, he will turn quite
naturally to the cholerics. He himself will impersonate by his manner
and delivery the strength and resolve of the character in question, and
his young cholerics will hardly be able to *hold* their seats. If his story
tells of a hunt or a chase or a pursuit of some kind, he will, with an
eye to his sanguines, develop such a rapid change of scene or multitude
of happenings that he out-sanguines the sanguines, so that they are
glad for a time to 'rest in peace'. For the melancholics he will select
matters of great detail, appeal to their marked thoughtfulness and their
long memories, and at the same time miss no opportunity to lead them
to forget themselves in entering into the griefs and trials of another.
With the phlegmatics the approach is always more difficult. A very
effective method is to select a high point in the story when all are
agog to go on, and then stop dead, silent, before them; in the sudden
hush they may begin to look up with a wondering eye, disturbed for
a moment out of their seeming somnolence, and then the teacher must
reach into them with force to impress, in that moment, all he can upon
their minds. Of course, these are mere hints at possibilities which
offer endless variations. Though the children are in groups they are
also individuals all the time, and the class teacher must know each
one well. He is rather like the conductor of an orchestra, now turning
to one group, and then immediately to another, and then again
signalling to the one or the other child within a group. Such lessons
have to be well prepared, with each child in mind. The whole class
is kept alive and moving. Then when the stories or descriptions are
retold on the next day, as they mostly are, he will know whom best
to call on at the one time or the other.

The grouping of the children according to temperament is not easy. It requires very careful observation of each child, not only in his general behaviour pattern but in the qualities of the work he produces. Sometimes a teacher will need the help of his colleagues to clarify his own picture. There is rarely, or perhaps one could say, never a pure one-temperament child. There may be a choleric-sanguine and that is not the same as a sanguine-choleric. There may even be a choleric-melancholic, or a melancholic concealing a choleric. Strangely enough there can also be a type of sanguine-phlegmatic, or a mixture of melancholic and phlegmatic.

Then, to make the matter more complicated, there is frequent evidence of an induced temperament. For example, in the case of broken homes the effect on a child might well be to induce a feeling of loss and abandonment and consequently of melancholy though not actually a melancholic. Or it may bring about a feeling of resentment, an inner mood of rebellion against circumstances, and this may induce irritability and anger in a child who is not by nature a choleric. Another child may, in self defence, build up an attitude of indifference—become a pseudo-phlegmatic. We need to develop a very sensitive regard for such matters.

To take another instance, the effect of television. The flood of impressions undoubtedly tends to produce sanguinity and lack of concentration, whilst the physical situation of being 'held' to the screen can result in a state of inner fixation akin in character to the phlegmatic.

The method of work described here applies more directly to younger children. As we approach the secondary school years the method may still be there though in a more subtle manner. There is often to be perceived an actual change of temperament in the passage 'from childhood to youth', that is, at the approach of adolescence. The reader may ask himself whether he might recall such a change in himself. And there are still other factors in an overall study of the subject.

Still to be considered with regard to the grouping of temperaments is the effect the children have on one another: the cholerics in a bunch, all equally ready to leap to the charge, might bring a somewhat sobering effect—choler balancing out choler; so too, several shifting changeable sanguines together, darting in mind from point to point (and in body too, if they could) might have a subduing effect on one another. And the melancholics together produce a curious effect—they cannot compete in weeping as the cholerics can in shouting or the sanguines in darting about; to be a weeper amongst weepers begins to become rather droll. The phlegmatics, each one so enclosed in himself, become uneasy in sensing themselves, each one, surrounded by so many silent blocks.

Altogether, the subject of temperaments, as we have shown, is a very serious one. Each temperament brought to an extreme results in its own type of mental illness, the maniac, the imbecile, the suicide, the silent sitter. This shows further how deep-rooted the temperaments are in human nature. And yet, in ordinary life, there is much room for humour, and the teacher certainly must conduct the matter with a light heart and a twinkling eye.

For a delightful description of children and their temperaments we warmly recommend *Childhood*[1] by Caroline von Heydebrand, a leading pioneer of the first Waldorf School in Stuttgart.

---

1 C. von Heydebrand *Childhood*, Rudolf Steiner Press, London 1988.

Chapter 6

ADOLESCENCE

With puberty we enter the third period of childhood. It may be compared in history to the passage from the middle ages into modern times—an entry into a totally new relationship with the world. Once again soul forces are released which were previously at work within the organism, this time more particularly from the rhythmic system; there is a further readjustment between body, soul and spirit. The forces which are now freed provide the basis for a personal life of feeling; for the first time life becomes a personal affair, an individual questioning of existence in all things big and small. It is not that younger children do not question and that the answers they receive do not directly concern them, but now the emphasis is more on thought. Subject confronts object far more sharply—the need to *justify* relationships, not merely to accept them, asserts itself. The wish arises to make one's life one's own.

The matter may be described in different ways. It is common today to speak of body, soul and mind; we, however, have preferred the term spirit. What is mind, and what is spirit? They are certainly not synonymous. Mind, etymologically, is connected with 'memory', spirit with 'breath'. Memory resides in each single soul, whereas breath is universal. Mind is fashioned according to personal history but spirit transcends history; yet mind is akin to spirit. We may say that in mind the personal life of soul grows aware of a realm of spiritual values reaching beyond it; soul is lifted into the realm of spirit and communes with it as a world apart from itself. The spirit, however, may be born *within* the mind as inward revelation. The human being will then know himself at one with the kingdom of the spirit and standing within it, even as a man knows himself within his skin and standing within the world of nature around him. In this way the spirit may know itself within the confines of personal mind yet transcending and reaching beyond it. The adolescent has not yet reached the stage at which this becomes possible—he is still to this extent a child. In him, however, the breath of the spirit may awaken a 'memory' of itself, a memory not of earth. This awakening to the inner self first expresses itself as the beginnings of an independent life of thought; it becomes a search through the idea for the 'ideal'—a longing, as Rudolf Steiner says, to discover that the world is based on truth. This longing for the ideal may take different forms: it may appear as a restlessness to leave school, enter life and become quickly an adult; it may be charged with romantic imaginings—'castles in the air'; it may be seized by vain ambitions or be driven by desires. Much will depend on background conditions and the education that went before. What thus awakens is, at its best, an inner dream of higher goals and possibilities. In the new questioning about life and in the personal search for truth which begins at this third stage of child development, we may recognize the first stirring of the spirit within the wakening mind of man.

In a real sense the adolescent begins to discover himself in the world of ideas. He *enjoys* ideas as the younger child enjoys pictures and the still younger child play. To begin with it is almost like a new game—the will to argue, to assert or to contradict opinions—but it is far more than that; this new life in self-sustained ideas is like stepping into a realm of freedom where the inner life of man first begins to experience its independent nature. Hence the demand for independence which, to the young adolescent, intoxicated with this sweet and liberating sense of freedom, seems so justified, and to the adult, who still views him as a child, so perplexing.

The adolescent begins to question all things: himself, the world, the authority of parent, of teacher, the meaning of destiny, the values of life or the value of life itself. It is a moment of release; yet it brings with it added loneliness. The following poem[1] by A.E. expresses this well.

AWAKENING

The lights shone down the street
In the long blue close of day:
A boy's heart beat sweet, sweet,
As it flowered in its dreamy clay.

---

1 With permission of A.M. Heath & Co., and acknowledgements to Mr. Diarmuid Russell.

Beyond the dazzling throng
And above the towers of men
The stars made him long, long,
To return to their light again.

They lit the wondrous years
And his heart within was gay;
But a life of tears, tears,
He had won for himself that day.

It may be objected that not all young people are poets and feel these
things so strongly. It would be truer to say they do not all feel as
clearly. Among young adolescents, however different they may be,
there is still a common bond which is very strong; they will rise up
in ready protest and indignation if this delicate sense of self, the birth
of the 'subject' within the mind, is in any way slighted or ignored.
Puberty means for all of them the end of naïve childhood and the
beginning of a life of personal endeavours, hopes, loves, problems,
sorrows and discontents which they now know they must eventually
resolve themselves. They are glad and thankful for a lead from one
whom their hearts can accept, and they love the man who can bring
them the seriousness they need and yet the relief of golden laughter.

A great help with discipline at this time is the art of gentle and
unprovocative humour; sarcasm, for example, can be most hurtful
and destructive. In adolescence, life becomes at one and the same
time universal and markedly personal; the newly awakened 'ideal'
element which wishes to discover truth in all the world finds itself
bound and hampered, and the impulse of love for all things confused
and fettered by desire. It is not for nothing that Milton, as a young
man, wrote both *L'Allegro* and *Il Penseroso*; youth is both gay and
melancholy. How can education help? The following description of
painting in our schools and the transition to black and white shaded
drawing will be one indication.

From the Nursery Class on there is a weekly painting lesson in water
colours. In the Nursery Class little more is done than to help the
children keep their colours bright and clean and flowing. The colours
are dissolved, and they paint with large square brushes on a moistened

surface. From the First Class on, the attempt is made to lead them into an experience of the specific qualities and inherent possibilities of the colours themselves. Just as the letters of the alphabet, limited in number, can yet build up words of innumerable meanings, so the colours, too, few as they are, may in their interplay express an infinitude of shades and qualities and moods. Colour studied in this way becomes a direct language of the soul. There is much stress laid today on self-expression; but there must be a conscious command of the self, a studied medium, something to express, and the required disciplines with which to express it: that alone is art. If children are left only to do as they will, what benefit can it be to them? Sooner or later it leads to a kind of exhaustion. Gifted children will always produce something interesting—for a time! Then they either fall into habits and mannerisms or grow empty. One gains the impression, at times, that with the self-expression enthusiasts anything 'odd' is accounted remarkable. There are many 'odd' corners in the human soul and the results are sometimes quite 'remarkable'. The only way to real freedom of expression is through careful schooling; this applies to art at all times and to children quite especially. A methodical training in the unique language qualities of the different colours; how they merge and interpenetrate to give *known* effects; how yellow of itself is radiant and expansive though it can densify to resting gold; how blue lends form, how it can hold and also lead into depth; how red can be power at rest, can mount to triumph or turn to anger; how colours can be warm or cold; how each colour has its range and yet how their effects can multiply like situations on a stage between the actors—such a study, through exercise, usage, long experience and discovery, gives the ground for freedom where self-expression finds a legitimate and positive outlet. Children need schooling in all things, and then, in the measure that they are schooled and given the right materials with which to work, their originality will gather force and find increasing range of expression. The colours on the page become moods and qualities in action, and the forms are not 'drawn in' but arise through the play of surfaces and the meeting of tone perspectives. This the young child learns through guidance and experience. The intention of the work is not to produce artists—artists will be artists anyway—but to train a generation of men disciplined through art, to quicken and educate the creative impulse in all children and, in the end, to carry youthful athleticism of soul into old age. If the poet has a young heart why should not all men have younger hearts? This is the mission of all the arts practised in our schools, each with its special skills and opportunities for training. There are people who still think that art is effeminate, especially for boys. Art is more powerful in life than concrete arches and steel bridges! Art carries life along. The soul expands through it to new dimensions.

At puberty the children cease to work with colour for a time and, instead, turn to black and white. This is a medium of sharp contrasts, well suited to the inner struggle of light and darkness, of personal conflict and resolve, into which they must now enter. The pictures they produce are eloquent of this. They vary very much with different children and yet have very much in common. One such picture may be of a dark, cloud-swept sky with a strong shaft of light breaking through; another of a storm-tossed ship with the haven of rest far ahead; yet another of a desolate landscape and in the background a hill with a cross or a chapel or an image of the Grail upon it; or perhaps just a solitary figure gazing pensively at nature or communing silently with itself. Frequently there is a human figure attacked by daemonic shapes of every kind, like the Temptation of St. Anthony, and, somewhere above or behind, a being like a guardian angel. These pictures reflect the inner mood; the particular subject chosen is only incidental to the mood. Results can be startlingly unexpected. Sometimes the same child will work through pictures of torment and horror and then, at the last, reach to something tender and sublime. After a year or two, when greater stability has been acquired, there is a return to colour, but to a more conscious use of it and, through the work in black and white, to a clearer appreciation of form.

In the matter of puberty our age is prone to exaggerate the part played by sex. To ignore it is foolish but to regard it, as many do, as the primary and determining factor in life is a gross error. It is not sufficiently observed how closely the *erotic* is allied to the *neurotic*: both are the consequences of over-intellectualism in the sphere of thought on the one hand and undernourishment of feeling on the other. The very fact that there is so much emphasis on 'sex' is itself evidence of the over-intellectualism which this education is trying to combat; soul-starvation is interpreted as sex-starvation.

The impulse of love is an all-embracing one—it would include the whole of existence; the impulse of love for all things also hallows the love for the particular. No one has expressed this more beautifully than Soloviev in his book *The Meaning of Love*. 'The meaning of human love, speaking generally, is the *justification and deliverance of individuality through the sacrifice of egoism*. On this general foundation we can also solve our particular problems to explain the meaning of sex-love.' It is our materialistic view of nature that makes the human soul a stranger in this world and flings man back emotionally upon himself and his desires; it is this with all its consequences that defeats the impulse of true love and reduces it to a sex episode. Where the spirit is awake and aware, sex is the detail and love the reality. The young adolescent in his newly discovered loneliness longs to find a world that is worthy of his love. He has the impulse to know life and to find in life the ideals he seeks. The following poem in translation is not written by a youth but by a modern poet, Iqbal.

LONELINESS

To the sea-shore I went and said to a restless wave,
'Thou art always in quest of something. What ails thee?
There are a thousand bright pearls in thy bosom,
But hast thou a heart like mine in thy breast?'
It merely trembled, sped away from the shore, and said nothing.
I betook myself to the presence of God, passing beyond the sun
    and the moon, and said:
'In the world not a single particle knows me,
The world has no heart, and this earthy being of mine is all heart.
The garden is charming, but is not worthy of my song.'
A smile came to his lips, and he said nothing.[1]

Young human beings long to find that the world has a heart. How easy it is today to give up the quest as foolish.

The adolescent wants to discover the true hero in man, the fighter for the ideals of the human race, for truth, beauty, goodness. The world we live in crucified Christ; this does not diminish, it glorifies the Christ Deed. So, too, there is no age, before or since the Christ

1 With permission of MacMillian & Co.

Event, without its heroes; they are not made less because the world rejects them or receives them tardily. How many prophets have not been ridiculed and persecuted here on this earth? The teacher who is himself filled with the quest for the true foundations of human existence; who sees clearly how man, in his essential being, contradicts and transcends all natural law; how he is called upon perpetually to war against the beast which would rob him of his manhood—how easy is the fall, how hard the ascent; how much, how very much depends upon a man keeping faith with himself—such a teacher will not be lacking in material to inspire and give heart to his pupils. The heroic calls to the heroic, and to learn to behold the hero in man is to waken the slumbering forces of heroism in human nature.

All external nature follows the given law; man alone lives by the law he sets himself. Nature reproduces itself but man is constantly producing the new and the unpredictable—he is the great enigma of our modern science because what he truly is escapes all outer scrutiny. The lion is a lion by virtue of its species; the more perfectly it embodies its species, the more perfect it is as a lion, and the same is true of all creatures and of all the kingdoms except the human kingdom; the ideal of the perfect man, however, is that he shall be the prototype of himself alone. Try as we will we cannot specify the individual man—our interest in him is roused to the extent that everything which is more general in his nature falls away; it is not man the species, but the uniqueness of each single man which reveals to us the true nature of man. The creature lives solely by instinct, but man ascends to free initiative, and this initiative, springing from the hidden sources of his manhood, adds ever new content to the sum total of existence. Man has lived through countless hours of darkness, treachery, disruption—through countless denials of himself and his Creator—yet the hero in man adds wonder upon wonder as revelation of the spirit. Egypt is a wonder. Greece is a wonder. Renaissance art is a wonder. These last centuries have produced many wonders. The Ninth Symphony is a wonder. So is the George Washington Bridge a wonder in its own degree, where complexity has been so far resolved that the law of its construction stands revealed in all its simple grandeur. We measure life by that which is creative in it, and as teachers we have the mission so to educate that the creative in man may find utterance; it may speak to us in many tongues and in many modes and still remains the language of man. Today we may point to many horrors which twist and distort the human countenance out of recognition, yet somewhere beneath the vileness we may still glimpse, disconsolate, beseeching, the face of man. As teachers we have to lead the vessel in our charge safely through the Scylla and Charybdis of modern times, egotism in material things and scepticism in spiritual things; the one makes too much of the earth, the other too little of heaven.

The passage to truth, the passage through the Scylla and Charybdis of today, is indeed a perilous one. The one temptation is to regard man as no more than a thing in a meaningless world; the other, to convince him that he is a nothingness in himself. In broad and in large these are the conclusions the world has arrived at, and it is with these that the teacher is expected to meet the youthful idealism and eager expectation of his adolescent pupils as they press on to prepare for their part in life.

How has this come about? For too long man has regarded himself as a detached spectator of the world of nature, quite forgetting that his own thoughts, perceptions, feelings, impulses and actions are not only an intrinsic but the most significant part of the world process in which he finds himself. He has failed to recognize that his knowledge of the world can only be commensurate with his knowledge of himself which, today, is approximately nil. What he knows of himself is the mechanism of his organism; analyse this organism as he will, it brings him no nearer to his true self. What he knows of the world is its mass-energy composition in meaningless and never-ending motion; try as he will, he can never come to terms with himself in such a world. Both ways he finds *himself* excluded; all meaning fails him. The whole of existence has been exhausted of meaning like a vacuum tube of air. What can a voice do in a vacuum, and what can a soul do in a meaningless void?

What has been achieved in this scientific age no one will deny. It is what has not been achieved which concerns us here. What has not been achieved is to arrive at a concept of man by which he can live. From a strictly scientific point of view, however complicated a thing a man may be, he is nevertheless a thing, and a thing can have no claim to being a *self*, far less a self-determining self. Beyond the concept of 'thing' some might prefer the term 'energy-complex'. If man should imagine himself more than a thing or an energy-complex, he lives in illusion.

This is the point of combat. Such concepts may serve for robots but not for men. They give the lie to all claims for higher truth and make life an absurdity. We demand faith from the young and in the same breath deprive them of the faith they have; we present ideals to them and nullify the ideals we present; we pose as responsible people who know the world and daily exhibit our irresponsibility. This, as seen through the eyes of youth, is devastating. Here lies the danger for the young: they must either accept our thesis that life has wants, desires, prospects of a sort but no meaning, or they must reject us and our thesis to seek their own unguided course.

Facts remain facts and contain the truths we seek. The theories men construct about the facts depend on how they see them. If they see only their material aspect, then they evolve materialistic theories. The application of these theories leads to results of a certain kind. If they saw differently, they would think differently, interpret differently and arrive at different kinds of results. All depends, in the first place, on the seeing. Rudolf Steiner beheld the same facts but saw them differently. His seeing led him to a spiritual view of the universe and man. Within the phenomena of nature he beheld a higher nature; within man, a higher man. He saw, and he taught others to see, that morality is a fact which has its roots in a spiritual world but blossoms through man in this one. Through man, also, earthly events acquire eternal meaning. He placed it as the greatest ideal of Waldorf education that the young people going through the schools and entering life might, in course of time, arrive of themselves at a worthy concept of man, one that would ennoble life instead of debasing it. This is the striving of the teachers also. It is not possible in so short a space to do more than hint broadly at the mood and character of the teaching in a Rudolf Steiner high school. The work is as strictly scientific as elsewhere but the phenomena are presented and viewed differently. It is man who occupies the central place in everything taught. Over against the cold analysis of facts as commonly presented, there is live attention to the constructive forces of human thought, feeling and imagination. The interpretive power of the heart is added to the analytical nature of the mind. This leads to the view that the world is a work of art and not a machine. It leads to the view that man is a synthesis of world creation: in him the physical and the moral, the natural and the divine, meet. Through his achievements creation advances further.

To take the adolescent through the history and development of art as the revelation of evolving manhood; to educate him into the meaning and appreciation of poetry as the medium wherein the centre in man finds kinship with the heart of all creation; to unfold the nature of love, by way of the great sagas and literatures of the human race, as the search of man for his own kingdom; to show that the ideals man carries are the earnest he has of his true estate, that there is conception in the spirit as well as in the body, that moral imagination is not a chimera of the mind but a power for renewing life; to discover that history follows a mighty plan of promise and fulfilment, that it leads from a state of moral and spiritual dependence towards the goal of self-mastery and self-determination, from community by descent in the past to community by assent; to demonstrate that nature has depth as well as surface and that as man grows in insight so will the ultimate goal of science be attained, the rediscovery of the divine; to come to an understanding of the spiritual heritage of the East and to an appreciation of the spiritual promise of the West; to see that men are made different in order that they may grow more greatly united; to perceive mankind, with Paul, as many-membered, but One Body filled with One Spirit; to learn to see warmly and to think humanely; to recognize the meaning of 'to die in order to live' and to see the many deaths that man must die to gain his immortality; to educate youth along such ways, positive towards others, resolute in oneself, careful in study, thoughtful in observation and self-expression, to pursue all this with enthusiasm and with faith in the attributes and striving qualities of man—to do this is to ennoble the mind, to fire the imagination, to fortify the will and to quicken initiative for life. To lay such seeds as may produce new vision and discovery in the years to come, this we regard as the primary task, the duty and the aim of an education worthy of its name. The task of the teacher is not to mould the mind but to enable it to grow to new dimensions—dimensions, perhaps, beyond his own reach. It is thus he serves the present for the future.

We have emphasized the ideals of a Rudolf Steiner education, but these ideals also include a meticulous care for simple and practical things, and they include the labour of overcoming difficulties. It is not merely that the new broom must sweep clean, it must sweep better than the last new broom. For example, the study of the steam engine will include not only the lives of its inventors and the obstacles they had to overcome both in the workshop and in public life, the resulting industrial revolution, the rise of new populations and their needs—it will also include painstaking draughtmanship, the basic physics required to understand what is technically involved, laboratory work, and good, clear notebooks, and—alas, for some—the unavoidable mathematics! But as a kind of compensation at least, there will be visits to industrial plants, to a locomotive shed, possibly even to a coal mine, and meetings and informal talks with the men who spend their lives in such work. Even here there may be more to learn than was altogether bargained for. I remember the young ladies of one party who chose to come out in all their Sunday best on a visit to a locomotive shed. It was an impressive sight! Well, they came out that way and they went in that way, but when they came out again— what a soiled and besooted company—but, at least, with purged and illumined souls! What a lifelong impression for these young people to learn from a man's own lips that he is prepared to stoke for seven long years before he can advance to become an engine driver!

Industrial visits are, for the young adolescents particularly, an important part of their social education. They want to know what kind of world they live in. A single visit down a coal mine, or to an iron foundry, or to an aluminium factory, opens a picture for them of modern industrial production, and also of the men and women engaged in it. To be making use of things all day long, as we do, merely as a matter of course without ever enquiring further as to who and what stands behind them is plainly egotistical. We switch on the light, we lift the receiver of the telephone, we press our foot down on the accelerator, all there for our convenience, with scarcely a thought for the human lives involved. On the other hand, such visits awaken a live interest in such matters, and with it a sense of indebtedness to all the countless human beings with their particular gifts and capacities and modes of service on whom our own lives depend. They may also help towards the realization of a persistent error in human thinking which is at the back of the industrial and social unrest of our times, one to which Rudolf Steiner drew attention earnestly, the idea that human labour, not just the work produced, can also be regarded as a commodity, that we can buy labour and even barter for it. Thus we confuse the value of a product which can be estimated with the inestimable character of the human gifts involved. I can pay for a pair of shoes but I can no more pay for the inventive power that designed them and the instruments involved or the skilled hands that finally shaped them than I can pay for the gift of poetry of the poet. The gifts by which human beings contribute to life can only be regarded reverently for they have their source elsewhere. To understand this, quite apart from the interest roused in the technological and practical aspects, is to·nurture seeds of genuine brotherhood, fraternity in economic life.

We recount a visit to a glass factory and what could be seen and learnt there. First, it is surprising to know that the smooth transparency of glass is derived from sand, the ultimate crumblings of what were once crystalline rocks—hence the transparency; then to see how the sand is smelted into a liquid, that glass in its nature is a liquid—it has been found, for example, that a pane of glass in an old building is slightly thicker at the bottom, that is to say the glass, however slowly, has nevertheless been in flow all the time. The liquid glass is so very malleable but it cools quickly into the brittleness of the solid state—as though the glass is ever ready to return to its first fragmented condition from which it derives. The greatest wonder, however, was to see the men, with their own body breath perfectly controlled, blowing the molten glass into the various shapes, here expanded, there contracted, larger or smaller at will—to perceive them with their marvellous skill and surety. They could determine, by varying their speeds of running, the relative widths of lengths of glass tubing down to a tenth of an inch or even finer. They had brought their skill right down into their legs, not only in their hands and breath. Here were craftsmen indeed, each casting a critical eye on his own handiwork before laying it aside for the next stage. Here was the pride of industry revealed at its best, in its most human aspect.

It was an old-fashioned plant, simply furnished, not too tidy, not even too clean—the work itself produced a. quantity of dust which the men must be careful not to inhale. There was an air of ease about the place though all were working hard. Pervading all was a happy mood of common interest, of fellowship, and of unstinting recognition of individual excellencies by the one for the other. The men were gracious to the young visitors, glad to answer their questions, and the latter were impressed, in addition to all else, with the fine quality of independence of the men, each one conscious of being a *master* in his own craft.

The same class, a day or two later, went to visit a highly modernized, super-hygienic chocolate factory. Here all was faultlessly spic and span. The women were bonneted, the men capped, and all aproned in meticulous white. These same figure were seated, at set distances apart, along a moving belt with its speed-controlled motion advancing the separate chocolates; each, as a chocolate passed him or her, had a single detailed action to advance the chocolate towards its final perfection. In that situation the people seemed no more than adjuncts of a mechanical system following its own given laws, a most strange impression after the freedom of the glass-workers. As a spectacle it did not feel right. Then, at a further stage, the chocolates were placed one by one in their assigned positions in the box, the lower layer, the covering, the upper layer and more covering, and finally the lid, the assembled package, the crate for the waiting lorries and the dispatch to all the countless confectioners in this and in many other countries—an endless chain system linking an endless number of lives in this one industry organized for luxury consumption.

But then came another aspect of that factory waiting to be seen, a theatre, common rooms, musical instruments, a gymnasium excellently equipped, facilities for indoor and outdoor sports, a buffet for social occasions, and all the signs of a great caring for the cultural welfare of the employees. One learned also of help with the schooling of the young, of college facilities for those who were capable, of care for the aged and the sick, a human counterpart to the system of automation witnessed previously. Every endeavour was being made to build up a social cultural community which, though not *visible* in the factory itself, was nevertheless there in the background, foster-ing a mood of warmth and fellow-feeling. There was no room for the pride of the individual craftsman, but maybe there was a shared satisfaction in the unity of purpose which pervaded the enterprise as a whole, an act of common service even though at the cost of individual sacrifice.

There were questions enough to be discussed in retrospect—foremost, the picture of human beings whose daily lives were so differently circumstanced, yet all engaged in service for the greater community at large. There was born, out of these visits, a feeling of profound respect for the services rendered and of gratitude to the people engaged in them. The young people had gained one or two vivid impressions of the industrialized society we live in, and maybe a heightened sense of responsibility for the services which they themselves, in course of time, would be rendering.

We do not overlook the fact that there is much in youth that is ungainly, crude, vain, selfish and foolish—in fact, that young people *can be very trying*, as the saying is. These very things, however, are better overcome, not by direct reproof but by indirect approach—by holding up the mirror of all that man, in his moral being, *may* become.

It is to be remembered that young people between fourteen and eighteen, that is, of high school age, can be sharply critical of the adults they meet and deeply disappointed in them. The younger ones expect to be understood even in their foibles and bravadoes and they often are not. Much of their play-acting is, after all, an attempt at asserting and testing out their first beginning sense of independent selfhood. They often feel badly misjudged. Why are these adults so dull, so self-contradictory, so lacking in humour? A youngster of fifteen in an American school declared in all seriousness that he knew what was wrong with the world, the adults were not really adult but only pretending to be so. Behind the assertiveness, flippancy and pointed disregard there may lie concealed great shyness, sensitivity, unsureness, even tenderness and a longing for a guiding hand which must be of their own choosing, but without which they can easily feel lost, abandoned, seeking refuge in a group or wandering off into what is often despairing loneliness. To win the confidence and affection of young people in their adolescent years is a beautiful experience for the teacher, but any direct attempt at gaining popularity will almost certainly have the opposite effect.

It is necessary that the young people should be active and practical; that they should make accurate as well as beautiful books; that they should carve and model and paint and practise various handicrafts—for such practice activates the will, educates the feelings and develops the perceptions. Music, drama, eurythmy, play a great part, and where possible Bothmer gymnastics. These activities are educative in a high degree and very necessary. Just because we live in an intellectual age, we need to pay all the more attention to an education of the will and to the achievement of a right intensity as well as balance in the life of feeling.

As for the social aspect at this stage, the children in the upper school have to learn to make their own adjustments amongst themselves as well as with the specialist teachers who now come forward to meet them. This stepping into the broader structure of the upper school and the encounter with a company of 'experts' in place of the one constant class teacher is the best possible acknowledgement of the fact that they have entered 'into a new age of life' and that all things henceforth must be different. Their social bearing changes rapidly.

It is a frequent subject of debate amongst educators of longer standing whether the youth of today are markedly different from those of ten, fifteen, twenty years ago. Most would agree that they definitely are different and there are some who claim that they find them more intelligent, original and generally more interesting. My own experience tells me that they feel themselves to be more adult; public life has to acknowledge this. Are they not now full-blown citizens at the age of eighteen—three years of former growing towards adulthood vanished in a flash? They are certainly traditionally less bound, more adventurous (also in matters of drugs, sex, far-distance travels, exotic teachings and practices). Yet withal, they are more fearfully uncertain of life, of death, of the future, and, in the same degree, more sensitively perceptive and therefore more open to spiritual impressions. The ground under their feet is thin. What feeling of security can they have? Has not the third world war already begun with all the frantic rivalry for ever more potent military missiles and effective counter-measures to keep the enemies at bay? Will the younger generation ever see peace? The chaos of uncertainties with old accepted standards rapidy vanishing and new standards not yet born—this reaches deeper into the soul than the mind can grasp. Life is dangerous and many young people live dangerously, and break down mentally, morally and physically. In schools and colleges they need to meet men and women who are at least one stride ahead, who are to that degree larger minded, larger hearted, larger visioned, inwardly compassionate, serious at need but capable of generous-hearted laughter. The problem where children are concerned comes back inevitably to the adult, above all to the teacher. If the young are different, life having so changed for them, what do we bring them that is new? By that we mean something new to live with, new hope, new promise, new as the springtime coming out of winter.

Chapter 7

WALDORF EDUCATION—IS IT STILL NEW?

Waldorf education, as we have seen, came into being in 1919, that is, over two generations ago. Since then there has been the Second World War and we have fully entered into a nuclear age. This means that the balance of life on this earth is vastly changed. Children are born and grow up in conditions that have never been more precarious and unpredictable. One symptom touching childhood most nearly lies in the widespread dissolution of the home and normal family life. In view of all this it may well be asked whether Waldorf education, from its beginning, has also changed with the times. To what extent can it still be regarded as a new art of education? What is new? The fact that it is spreading faster than ever across all language barriers gives sure evidence that it is felt to belong to the present time and that it is hailed by many as having something new. On what is this based?

We know that Waldorf education is born of the conception of man as a threefold being. That he thinks, feels and wills; that he is head, heart and limb, is taken to be obvious. Even that he consists of body, mind (rather than soul) and spirit, though those terms need clearer definition, is widely accepted. Yet it can hardly be said that these distinctions have entered deeply into educational practice. There the intellectual approach has grown more dominant at all levels. Note the importance attached to the intelligence quota as though the child is predominantly head, and the stress on exams as the all-deciding factor. Because education is directed head-wise down to the youngest children we no longer know clearly when infant becomes child, child youth, and youth adult. This in the end is not only confusing but can be disruptive.

Waldorf education, by contrast, makes a strong division between the infant years leading up to the change of teeth, the childhood years proper between the change of teeth and puberty, and the very marked changes in the youthful years following puberty. If the education is clear in this, then the transitions from the one phase to the other is also clear, and the curriculum and the treatment of subjects are ordered accordingly. It is this distinction between Waldorf and other schools that struck the inspectors so forcibly.

The head-wise approach, as we have called it, has serious consequences. Is the child brainy, will he be able to pass the exams, are for the parents dreaded questions. The non-exam child, the child in whom heart and limb do not keep pace with the head, comes to be looked on as inferior. Art and the crafts play second place. Thus all the three phases, infant, child and adolescent, are pressed forward intellectually and this has consequence for the whole of life. The clever ones are extolled, but where are the artists and the craftsmen who embellish life and give it greater quality? They are rare to find.

But the effects of over-emphasis on head or brain learning goes further than this. We see how the children in the kindergarten lose their spontaneous genius for play. They grow restless, are bored, or get uncontrolled, and then it needs adults with their thought-out games and learning devices to engage and entertain them. What belongs properly to the first years of schooling is pushed down into the pre-school years. That means drawing them into their nervous system, making them 'heady' too soon; but that means also robbing them of their early powers of phantasy, the source, if allowed to play itself out naturally, of greater creativity in later life. Then, as is seen so clearly in public life, we arrive at adults who fall short of demand, who cannot enter with imagination into the problems, mainly human problems, that confront them, and therefore cannot arrive at the needed solutions. Instead they make compromises which never are solutions. Such situations are all too familiar; that they might be the consequences of misused or misunderstood early childhood is scarcely dreamed of.

The same intellectually directed attitude plays as strongly into the elementary school years. We cannot wait long enough with reading, writing and arithmetic and there the slow and often more imaginative child who needs longer time comes off badly. Our public education, throughout the world, is imbued with this impatience for head-learning. Even if known, it is not accepted seriously that one is inducing prematurity of body, and therefore early puberty, or, in others, states of pre-adolescence with demands for freedom which do not belong to that age. This hinders or foreshadows the time for the healthy unfolding of the heart forces, so that people later do not know how to meet one another. They tend to remain lonely, isolated figures, too caught or engrossed in themselves. Loneliness has been described as the greatest malady of our time, leading also to excesses. There is much talk of community but little notion of sharing. So, too, parents are often at a loss to know how to meet their children.

The intellectualizing process through the school years finds its culmination in the examination system designed for the upper school. Here the examination programme with its prescribed choice of subjects, each with its given selected requirements, takes final charge of the situation, just at the time when the young people are awakening to a deeper questioning of life and its meaning. They are ready to recognize and be inspired by the ideals by which others have lived and are living. They are open to appreciate the great gifts of music, poetry and art as part of themselves, and the range of love in its manifold expressions, love for the world in all its beauty and mystery—but this falls outside the requirements; there is no room for it. What matters is the exam, the only entry to higher education and the better job, it is hoped, at the end of it. By great good fortune there may be a teacher, here and there, ready to share out of their own love and nobler aspirations something of what they have with their students. This can be a precious gift running through the whole of life. One looks back to it with gratitude as an act of grace—but that is something human, beyond the system. In the main, learning for exams hinders the free unfolding of the mind.

Working from the head down instead of, as is practised in the Waldorf schools, from the limbs to the heart to the head, one is in danger of countering the natural devotion of the little child contained in its power of imitation of the adult world round it—that which later becomes reverence for the whole of life. So, too, we fail to engender, as we should, the refining, and healing, and joy in beauty of the elementary school years. Likewise we can so easily neglect or misread the unfolding life of imagination and the latent idealism of youth, lending force to initiative in the years to follow. And thus we defeat, with our one-sided intellectualism, from phase to phase, the intuitive life of will, the inspirational life of feeling, and the imaginative life of thought, and arrive at a generation of depleted individuals suffering from a sense of unfulfilment and the feeling that they are not their real selves. These are the dangers. We need only look with an open eye at the world as it meets us and admit our own insufficiencies to see how inescapably true this is. It required a Huxley and an Orwell, but also many who have not written it down in books, to see the drift, through a kind of inner helplessness, towards world dictatorship in one form or another and the defeat of the free-born individual, but that also spells an inner death.

This danger Rudolf Steiner foresaw very clearly when he was developing his ideas for a threefold commonwealth, presenting the opposite trend, through a right interpretation of Liberty, Equality, Fraternity, towards an enlightened and morally free society, ideas that are implicit, at the educational level, in Waldorf education.

Hence to the adult he could say, extending an ancient word, 'Know thyself in body, soul and spirit,' or, in the life of will, feeling and thought, or, going further still, in religion, art and science—in the threefold aspect of human nature, the three-in-one.

Religion as intended here is in no sense denominational but which by its nature is all-human. So, too, art is not personal or subjective but that which reveals the whole of nature and creation as a work of art. By science is meant a knowledge that is all inclusive, where religion and art also bring their evidences—a total survey of truth with a genuine place in it for man. Present-day science has no place in it for man—it leaves him a homeless wanderer on earth.

Turning to childhood and the goals of education, Rudolf Steiner could say:

The unconscious ideal of the early child is that the world is built on goodness.

The unconscious ideal in the elementary school years is that the world is built on beauty.

The unconscious ideal of youth is that the world is built on truth.

Thus goodness, beauty, truth are not ideals imbibed from outside but they are the inborn shaping forces of human nature. If recognized and helped they lead to self-realization at the highest level as the guiding principle for every human being.

These are the guiding ideals of Waldorf education to be cast into a practical form leading to practical results. To the extent that such ideals are realizable in service to the future and the well-being of man, we may see that Waldorf education is as new and far-reaching today as on the day that Rudolf Steiner launched it into the world.

Chapter 8

QUESTIONS—
GENERAL AND PARTICULAR

The following are questions which recur frequently at interviews and after lectures. They will serve to illustrate a number of points connected with this education which have not been dealt with in the previous pages.

The Main Lesson
The day in a Rudolf Steiner school opens with a Main Lesson which lasts approximately two hours—a very long time, it would seem, but, in the way the lessons are arranged, it passes soon enough. The Main Lesson time is devoted to the main cultural subjects, Mathematics, English, History, Geography, Science and so on, and these subjects are taught in block periods of three or four weeks each. This calls for further explanation.

First, with regard to the two hours. The child needs time both to receive and to give. The teacher arranges the morning period so as to allow for this: to begin with, the children will be engaged in *listening*, be it to a story, a description, or whatever else is being presented as new content; there is a natural limit to this, and presently they will be standing reciting, or moving round the room clapping and stamping out their tables, or doing other forms of rhythmic exercise; then, towards the end of the lesson, there comes the time when they will be found busy on some form of individual work, maybe writing, drawing, modelling or whatever the particular main lesson subject happens to require. Thus the receptive and the active forces find their balance in the course of each lesson; thought, feeling and will receive their due share, and this, in the course of years, builds up a sense of health, security and general well being. The procedure described will vary with age and subject, but the essential aim is maintained, namely, that the child shall be exercised in all his faculties.

This finds amplification over the course of days. It is easy to observe how the experiences of the day settle into sleep, and how sleep *adds* something. Sleep is by no means merely the annulment of the day. In earlier epochs people knew this very well; they *addressed* themselves to sleep with trust and confidence—for them it was the portal of entry to those higher spheres whence they felt they derived their being and their daily strength and inspiration. Sleep leads through a positive process; the experiences of the day are carried down and established in the deeper-lying regions of the soul. By way of sleep, what is received during the day is woven into habits and condensed to faculties; chaotic living disturbs and disrupts this process, whilst bad and barren living bring emptiness of soul. The hygiene of sleep needs to become a direct concern of education. The process of learning is an assimilative one and follows a definite course. What is absorbed through observation and thought by day sinks into deeper strata of the soul at night and returns to consciousness confirmed in feeling and in will. This is a three-day process. What is taught on the one day is recalled in conversation on the second day and assembled, written down and given its final form on the third day. What is merely apprehended on the first day returns enriched by personal feeling on the second day and becomes part of oneself by the third day. This may sound strange at a first hearing but, once the attention has been drawn to it, practice will soon corroborate its truth. Of course, what is taught must engage the feelings and stir the will in the first place, but if it does, then, in the manner described, it acquires personal value and meaning for life. It is through observations of this kind that Rudolf Steiner leads education from speculative theory to human concreteness. He goes further and shows how what is taught reaches into the rhythmic functioning of the organism on the first night and into the metabolism process on the second night. It is thus that the soul faculties of thought, feeling and will are directly connected with the bodily processes in the nerve and sense organization, the respiratory and circulatory system, and the system of digestion and metabolism. It is because of this intimate connection that soul impressions can so directly affect body functioning and that body conditions are so easily reflected in the life of the soul, the more so the younger the child. This three-day cycle gives an extended view of the two-hour main lesson, in which the children partly learn, partly enter into rhythm, and partly into individual action. It should be noted that the rhythmic element includes the art of conversation with its give and take across the classroom; Rudolf Steiner attached particular importance to this. Thus the lesson, in it organic structure, attends to head and heart and limb, and includes the fact of sleep bringing order into the life of soul. Our children of today, living as they do in a welter of unrelated sense-impressions, and subject to all manner of irrelevant suggestion from the environment, *need* this help more than at any other time in history.

Added to this, continuation with the same subject over a period of weeks induces a mood of quiet and cumulative concentration; it deepens learning and integrates knowledge instead of departmentaliz-ing it—the example given of the steam engine could be extended to many others.

The class teacher knows when his children have reached saturation point in a given subject and when it is desirable, therefore, to turn to a new one. He arranges the subjects over the course of the year so as to provide for the best sequence, a more theoretical subject being followed by a more imaginative one, and so on. He also takes into consideration the time and season of the year. The beginning of a new lesson period becomes an event in a child's life. As text books are rarely used, never with young children, the issue of a new main lesson notebook always brings a thrill. Presently it will contain the child's own record of the new work done in class. In the youngest classes the teacher provides most of the text and the children illustrate. As they get older, the books become more and more their own handi-craft and the results are as individual as the children themselves.

It is often asked whether, on this block system, the children remember sufficiently what they have learned, for the same subject may not be taken again for the space of a whole year. It is largely a question of method. If the teacher takes the trouble, at the end of each morning, to recapitulate briefly the ground covered that morning, the same at the end of each week, and again at the end of the whole block period, it is surprising how much may be recalled even after a lapse of years. To forget for a time is a health-giving fact. Forgetting and remembering have been likened to going to sleep and waking again. What is recalled in memory is no longer a merely mechanical repetition of the past but has meanwhile been digested, assimilated and transformed through the child's own forces. It is an ideal of this education that the knowledge imparted should become substance for life, that it should grow by unseen ways, like life itself, into sustaining wisdom. If the lessons are not intellectual only, if they are imbued with imagination, if the child has received them gladly, if quite literally the life-blood has been stirred by them, and if then they are allowed to sink away, to be 'forgotten' for a time, then, when recalled, they have become *experience*. If, however, instead of description and characterization we feed the child on definitions and ready-made conclusions, if the object of teaching is that things should never be forgotten but should be retained in the same form all through life, we load the mind with unassimilable bodies, with stones instead of bread. The main lesson period if rightly given achieves permanence in the child's life by way of life itself; it *grows* and evolves with the child.

The system of main lessons continues right through the school. In the elementary school the sequence of subjects in the course of the year and the time allotted to each are matters which each class teacher works out in relation to his class. In the high school this is taken over by the specialist teachers who work this out by mutual agreement.

Religion In Our Schools

Questions are often asked about religion. There are parents who fear their child may be influenced before he arrives at his own free judgment; there are others of various religious persuasions who are concerned lest their child should be alienated from them by meeting a different kind of teaching.

As for the agnostic or free-thinking parent, a realistic view of history will show that all notable forms of human culture lead back to a religious source. It follows, therefore, if child development has as its background human development generally, that religion must play some part in it. No child can suffer through having his thoughts and feelings raised to the highest expressions of the good whether in thought or picture. It is surely one of the greatest blessings in a child's life to have been able to experience reverence, devotion and awe, and to have learned to recognize how these qualities have lived in the greatest teachers of all times. Moreover, it is an illusion to think that a child can be left 'free'. The child is above all impressionable—on that all will agree. If we do not guide him positively, but leave him 'free', he merely falls subject to all the day-to-day influences that come sweeping down on him. The unmeaning and destructive nonsense which meets him everywhere then takes possession of his mind, undermining faith faster than it can be built up. There is everything to be said for children having what really belongs to them—and childhood faith and reverence and religious feeling most certainly belong as part of their need.

And as for the parents with a religious concern, it may be said that the Christian attitude implicit in the life of our schools is one which pertains to all men and is in no way sectarian or bigoted. By the very fact that history is led back to the great mythologies we already draw near to the religions of the different peoples. The Old Testament, as was seen, has a special place even in the main lesson work. But Hinduism, Buddhism, the Muslim religion, and all that has come down from Persia, Egypt, Greece, Norse culture, ancient China, the world of America before Columbus—all these form part of the total story of man, and each is given its due. Nevertheless the Christ Event in its dynamic and evolutionary aspect is looked upon as the fulcral centre of all that story, seen in its intimate connection with the advance to ego-consciousness typical of the whole human race. This is a view that transcends that of any particular religion, for it has room for all of them, yet paying due reverence and regard to each. Religion lessons are given in most of our schools, in some side by side with those of denominational teachers who come expressly for that purpose. In many of the schools there are also Sunday Services, taken by the religion teachers and attended by those children whose parents wish it. In the last resort, however, it is recognized that the question of personal religion as related to a given Church or creed belongs essentially to the home.

Circumstances differ in different countries. In the original Waldorf School, according to custom in that area, pastors of the different denominations came to the school to collect the children of their congregations for separate religious instruction. Then some of the parents approached Rudolf Steiner and asked him if their children might have special non-denominational religion lessons with teachers of the school. Thus, side by side with the already existing arrangements, there were introduced what came to be known as the 'free religion lessons'. In England the usual practice being for teachers rather than pastors to take the religion lessons, this was also followed in the Waldorf schools. In America, religious instruction is not permitted in the state (public) schools, and though this restriction does not apply to private and independent schools it raises a special problem. Whatever the conditions, each school is free to make its own decision in this matter. There is no set policy of any kind.

Eurythmy

A word about eurythmy, which plays an important part in all our schools. This is an art of movement founded by Rudolf Steiner. Like all the other arts, it has its special contribution. It is based on language and on tone and has been described as 'visible speech and song'.

If man were not constituted for language he would never speak or utter poetry; if he were not fashioned according to musical law, he would never sing or produce the art of music. Culture in every form is an externalization of man himself, the created man becoming in turn creative. Just as he himself is composed according to law, so the art he produces must be obedient to law. He bears architecture within him, is a sculptured form, dwells in colour and stands as image in the world; so, too, the plastic arts of his making resolve themselves into imagery. But man is not static, he has his being in time; he moves, and produces sounds out of his inward nature, and so his poetry and his music are 'flowing arts', released into space but moving in time. The plastic arts have been described as frozen music, the musical arts as form dissolved. Eurythmy makes the flow in time visible in space. Being an art, it must be exact; composed of gestures, each gesture must have precise meaning, in no way less precise than the consonant or vowel, tone or interval, which it portrays. Just as each sound of a language or each tone in music offers a great variety of nuances according to context, so has the corresponding gesture in eurythmy equal variety of expression; nothing in eurythmy is arbitrary. It is the interpretative act of the artist, subject to discipline and law, which constitutes an art. Since language is laden with thought, imbued with feeling, spun to action, eurythmy must be capable of interpreting all these; also past, present and future; epic, lyric and dramatic; the serious and the burlesque, and so on. So, too, in music eurythmy brings to view melody, harmony, beat; major and minor; the qualities of the different keys; the mood or the changing moods of a composition; the orchestration of a piece. The training includes exercises of every kind, for skills, rhythms, alertness and sudden change, or the social interdependence of a group. Translated into classroom education, all this is excellent for children. Much that we have described as 'harmonizing' finds support and direct application in eurythmy. Moreover, the movements reflect man's higher attributes and are ennobling in themselves.

Discipline

What is your attitude to discipline? For example, 'Spare the rod and spoil the child!'?

Discipline in a Waldorf school is neither rigid in the traditional sense nor free in the progressive sense. The discipline aimed at is one where there is an easy, peaceful atmosphere in which all can breathe freely. This arises quite naturally where there is the right human understanding between the teacher and his children, a caring concern met by affectionate regard. A good teacher has his own kind of discipline just as he has his own method of teaching—the two go together. One that is lacking in experience may be hard put to it for a time; if he can learn to retain his calm in class and to take himself to task at home, he is most likely to find his way; if, however, he cannot master his problem, he is probably no teacher. On the other hand where there are actual trouble makers, it becomes a question of finding and remedying the cause. Why should a certain child be ill-mannered, rebellious, over-sanguine, destructive, or generally provocative? The cause may lie in the home, in experiences at a previous school, or in a condition of health—bad sleep, for example—or in some form of maladjustment either *in* the child or due to his surroundings (excessive exposure to television, for example, and, in our view, for the young child all television is excessive). These are matters for careful study and diagnosis on the part of all concerned, teachers, parents, doctor. Then therapy must follow, if possible in co-operation with the home. There must be an ill cause somewhere; this needs to be discovered. To say a child who lies or steals therefore needs the birch or its equivalent is a poor attitude on the part of education, though many still claim it to be a good one. In England there was (maybe still is) a society for the abolition of corporal punishment and another similar society for its preservation. From time to time these two societies would arrange joint meetings. The opposing parties sat facing each other across the floor. The discussions were interspersed, in parliamentary fashion, with loud cat-calls and other appropriate noises and often with volleys of mutual abuse. Correction there must be naturally—and not by mere remonstrances but by action. Stories have often helped with younger children. The type of action must be suited to the child and to the offence. Sometimes a play specially written for a child has worked wonders. Or, again, a task carried out faithfully over a period of time, days or weeks, in which the teacher has had the will to participate from start to finish, may work a change for life. The following examples will illustrate this further.

We instance the case of a child who resisted growing up; at every stage requiring a forward step in consciousness, she held back. She was slow with reading, number work, grammar, composition and the rest but excelled in painting, drawing and handwork, always, however, at a 'younger' level than her class. Socially, she was an active, lively child, liked by her class-mates, but she insisted on remaining 'young'. At the approach to puberty, when the thought forces should grow more independent, all this took a curious form. She longed to leave school as soon as possible. Outside school, she began to ape the grownups round her by an assiduous use of cosmetics, and her dream was to work in a beauty parlour. Then, however, she began also to take other people's purses and to acquire in this way a private source of wealth. When questioned about this she could, with a disarming show of candour and innocence, invent the most ingenious explanations on the spot. Her inventiveness was extraordinary. It might have been called lying, but actually she was only exploiting a gift of fantasy beyond its time. She had remained too bound to her child organism; the thought forces would not release. Not being able to take the forward step in thought which would have meant a real step towards growing up, she tried to make compensation in other ways: she imagined herself already in the world, she painted her face in adult fashion, she began to gather money (a perverse idea of freedom) instead of ideas. She really was innocent and a child despite her lying and her thefts. To have attempted to moralize or to punish would have been quite wrong. It was necessary to make a strong effort to bring more activity into her thinking, not by intellectual means but through her limbs: special eurythmy and other exercises were of great help.

In the two years which followed, these symptoms disappeared. When she left school, she tried out various forms of employment, discovered the way she wanted to go, and became what she had always promised to become—a bright, cheerful, warm-hearted individual with a strong caring for others. Had she been misunderstood at a critical time, and had discipline been other than a therapy, her case might have turned out very differently.

We quote another instance. A young boy suffered the death of his father whom he had greatly loved. About the same time, he had a severe internal operation. Further, he had been trained at a former school to be ambidextrous so that he scarely knew his right hand from his left. These various circumstances had produced a state of mental and emotional confusion and fear. His mind ran on many things but he could not concentrate, and the less he was able to do, the more despondent he became. He was witty and tried to engage his fellows by wisecracks and mischievous pranks. He could be hilarious one moment and lapse into tears the next. He had a gentle, loving disposition. In a mute way he showed his longing to be made whole of his several hurts.

The German language teacher, having consulted the class teacher, decided to give him the main rôle in a play based on the legend of St. Christopher. He was to be Offerus. Offerus was big and strong, determined to serve the strongest master. He therefore set out on a journey to find him. He was led to a mighty king and became a member of his bodyguard. Long did he serve him faithfully and well. Then, one day, there came a minstrel to the court. In the song he made mention of the devil. Offerus observed the king hastily cross himself with a look of fear in his eyes. So the king was not the strongest master. Offerus sought out the devil, which was not difficult. He hired himself out to the devil, wore black armour, and rode a black horse. Seven long years he served the devil faithfully and well. Then, one day, they were passing a wayside shrine, and Offerus saw the devil swerve to the side so violently that he almost fell off his horse. So the devil was not the strongest master. Offerus gave him back his black armour and his black horse and set off all over again in search of the strongest master.

One day he came to a hermitage where dwelt an ancient hermit. Offerus bowed to the hermit and said, 'Tell me, how can I find the strongest master?' The hermit replied, 'Only through fasting and prayer can you hope to find the strongest master.' Said Offerus, 'That does not suit me at all. Is there no other way?' 'Yes, there is,' said the hermit. 'Listen well, I will show you a path to follow. It will bring you to the bank of a great river. There you must build yourself a hut and dwell in it. Then, whenever anyone calls, you must carry them across the river.' So Offerus thanked the hermit, followed the path and came to the river. There he built himself a hut and lived in it and waited. Whenever anyone called he went and carried him across the river.

Years passed by and Offerus was old now, but never a sign did he have of the strongest master. One night he had lain down to rest when he heard a call. He went out to look but he saw nothing. Again he lay down to rest and again he heard a call. He rose and looked and saw nothing. Still a third time he heard the call and went out into the night. It was black, yet it seemed to him he could dimly see a child on the opposite bank. The voice that called was that of a child. Being now old he had made himself a stout staff to help him in his going back and forth across the river. He now fetched his staff and went across. It was indeed a child that he lifted on to his shoulder. As he journeyed back through the water, the child grew heavier and heavier till Offerus could scarcely take a further step. About half way across he stumbled. 'Who art thou?' he cried. And he heard the voice say, 'Know that you are carrying on your back the whole world, and not only the world but the Lord of the world as well.' At that moment he fell forward so that his head sank below the water, and the voice continued, 'Henceforth your name shall not be Offerus. Henceforth you will be known for all time as Saint Christopher, the Christ bearer.' And so he rose, Saint Christopher, and reached and entered the hut. The child had vanished and he fell into a deep sleep. When he woke his eyes beheld growing on his old and gnarled staff a spray of pure white blossoms. Then he knew for certain that he had at last met the strongest master.

It was astonishing to see this child, at that time only nine or ten, grow into his part—how memory, confidence, clarity and strength of gesture all improved. He never turned back. By degrees he made good his deficiencies. In course of time, he himself became a teacher. It may be said that the staff of St. Christopher never left his hand.

He could easily have been considered a general nuisance but 'the rod' would surely not have been his cure.

The third case to be quoted is a more obvious one. It concerns a rampageous boy who had been badly pampered and spoiled and who felt himself to be no end of a lad. He could be unruly and was always showing off. It is often the pampered child who feels particularly misused and grows most critical of the adults. On one occasion this boy, in his careless boisterousness, broke an object in a classroom. This time it was the woodwork teacher who took him to task. He had him back at school several times a week for several weeks. This, in itself, had a marked effect. Why should this busy teacher be so ready to punish himself for his sake? A human contact was made. With the teacher's help, the boy constructed a difficult piece of furniture that had long been needed in the classroom. There came the day when, without comment, it was placed in position to serve the community of the whole class. This treatment, too, had an astonishing effect.

One further example, again different in kind, will have to suffice. It is not easy for a newcomer to find his way into a well-established class. This is perhaps particularly the case in a Waldorf School, where each class, continuously from year to year, becomes a well-knit unit under the aegis of the class teacher. A new arrival alters the social structure of the class. Much devolves on the class teacher how the new member is received and integrated.

There was the case of a lad who had come from a totally different environment and who found it specially difficult to adjust. He felt he had to make his mark somehow and he did it in a very curious way: a curious art of 'spitting'. It was not that he expectorated violently in the way his grandfather might have done into the parlour spittoon. His was a far more delicate performance. In a given moment—what determined the moment was never properly discovered, unless it was that he suddenly felt forgotten—in such a moment he would purse his lips together, look around, discover his mark and fire his shot. True there was far more noise involved than actual substance, yet a modicum of substance there had to be to give support to the noise. Then he would raise his head and, with an expectant look in his face, he waited to see what might happen. This was a new phenomenon in the class which took the other children by surprise. They, too, waited, no less, to see what might happen. What happened was that there was a silent pause and then nothing happened. This was clearly a matter of disappointment to the boy who was so wanting to bring the focus of attention on to himself. He presently tried again and, indeed, a number of times and still nothing happened—possibly because the teacher himself was taken aback and did not quite know how to react. However, after a day or two of repeat performances, the teacher arrived in the morning with a large pail which he silently placed into the boy's hands. He then made a little speech about the widespread habit of spitting among certain types of animals, snails for example. Cats also have a kind of hiss and spit process when confronted suddenly by an aggressive dog—a strange mode of self-defence intended, however ineffectually, to ward off the enemy. He had also read or been told that toads spit. In the case of such animals there is always a discoverable cause, but there seems to be no evidence at all why boys should spit, certainly not in the case of a particular boy we were thinking about. Of course we would not wish to deprive him of his habit if that was going to be a real trouble to him. That is why he, the teacher, had brought the pail along for the boy's convenience. He had placed a second pail just outside the door in case it should be needed. There was only one request that he should get it over and done with right away so as not to interrupt the lessons later. Please would he go ahead as hard as he could. Needless to say, there was not a drier mouth in the whole of Christendom. An indescribable look of surprise came into that boy's face followed by a foolish sort of grin to the giggling but good-humoured amusement of the other children. There the matter ended.

Surprise is a most valuable element in education, and, of course, humour also. As for the boy, he had had his fling and come out the wiser. He turned out to be a very sweet-tempered and well-disposed individual. With the help of the teacher he had made a very good-humoured entry into the community of the class.

So one could go on. The main point is that discipline consists not only in maintaining outer order but in helping children to master their internal disorder, that it has to be therapeutic and constructive. A punishment that is to be worth while for the child invariably puts a burden on the teacher. A punishment which is automatic and which costs the teacher nothing has no moral value; at most it serves as a constraint—it may compel but it cannot transform. Discipline is an art which each teacher has to master in his own way.

The problem of discipline cannot be evaded. Nor does it leave room for half-measures; part-success is generally no success. The aim however must be a healing rather than a punitive one. If it is seen that despite all effort a child is not helped, parents and teachers may have to agree that a change is necessary—possibly a change of environment or even a period in a 'special school'. There have been such instances. In any case, bad discipline is inadmissible—it is bad for the child concerned and bad for the school. Let it be remembered that the core of true discipline is willing discipleship—but this cannot be demanded, it has to be won. Experience has shown how well this form of education favours this.

It should be added, however, as a warning to all, parents and teachers alike, that conferences held in many places of late confirm the view that 'disturbed conditions' in children have much increased, partly as the aftermath of war, partly as the reflection of the disturbed conditions of the times, and partly due to the amount of distraction that besets the young. Good growing demands peace; if this is true of a plant, it cannot be less true of man. Where there is peace of heart and mind, peace in the home and peace in the school, the kind of discipline for which we aspire comes naturally.

Games

What is your attitude to games? Most Rudolf Steiner schools provide the customary games, though they may have their preferences. Games, however, are played as games for the exercise and fun that they provide; no special ethic attaches to them nor is the capable player selected for special hero-worship. He is admired for his good achievement as is the good craftsman, the good actor, the good musician, the good at anything; no disgrace to one who cannot play. There are children with a natural dislike for organized games and they should be considered too and a suitable alternative found for them. But our children, when they do play, are known to play well and generally hold their own against competitors. They carry into their games the poise, agility and enthusiasm won from other activities.

It is often said that games provide a necessary outlet for the will; to the extent that this is true, it applies to our schools where the children have so much more scope for creative activity. Be that as it may, the simple fact remains that most children like games and should be able to have them, within reason and under good conditions. In so far as games are played at all in a Waldorf School, for the sake of the general morale it is important that teachers should learn to take a genuine interest in them and share in the enthusiasm of the children. Resentment grows in the children if teachers hold aloof and merely allow games to go on. They can, however, also be over-stressed, especially in the West, and have false ethical values attached to them. To learn to 'play the game' should be as simple as the words denote. Riding, swimming, boating and other such sports are encouraged where possible—also general outings and camping.

Transfer To Another School

Parents wishing to enter their children into a Waldorf School are sometimes concerned about what would happen if they had to leave the district and their children had to go to another type of school. Would they find themselves handicapped in any way?

At the outbreak of the war, Michael Hall was evacuated from London to Somerset and lost a hundred children. Some of these children could be followed up later. The general pattern was much the same. Not having been drilled in the usual intellectual way, and having followed a curriculum which does not run parallel to that in other schools, some of these children found themselves, to begin with, at a disadvantage. Then, however, their freshness and liveliness of interest took over and most of them went ahead surprisingly well.

Again, before the Rudolf Steiner School in New York had its own High School, children left at the seventh or eighth grade or even earlier for entry to the high school of their choice. Their record of achievement was greatly encouraging. With few exceptions they did very well, often even better than might have been expected of them.

The reason is the same. This education releases capacities, keeps the mind and imagination fresh, and wakens life interests. These qualities the children take with them wherever they go; they mark them out as good students.

Transfer From Another School

How late do you take children into your schools? The answer to this is: up to almost any age depending on the child. Though naturally the younger the better, there have been instances of children joining as late as the tenth or even the eleventh class who have quickly found the school to be their home and done well in it. There is this to be said. Children who arrive over-formalized may, for a time, seem to lose their bearings; they do not know how to gauge the type of self-discipline, both in conduct and in work, which is required of them. Help is here needed. In the main, the new type of demand and the relationship which exists between teacher and child bring happiness and release. Much that was previously unused is called into play. Often it is the late newcomers who appreciate what the school means to them better than do others who might never have been to any other type of school. It is not a question of doubting the excellencies to be found in other schools, but rather of pointing to the fact that the understanding for the child and his needs is different.

Entry Into Life

It is sometimes feared that children from these schools might find it specially difficult to adjust to life as it ordinarily is today. Are not the ideals in your schools unsettling for the tough business of everyday life?

Experience has proved the contrary. It is not to be gainsaid that first experiences may, sometimes, come a little hard, but, both during the war and since, old scholars have shown themselves very well able to meet difficult and shifting circumstances, to retain their presence of mind under stress, and to take initiative in the situations which they meet.

At a discussion amongst old scholars on what their school might have done for them, one of them declared: 'In my opinion, the education I received has definitely made life harder rather than easier, but this is just what I would not wish to have missed for it has taught me what real living means.'

Speaking generally, the old scholars of these schools are open-minded and much interested in the world around them and in people. Out of their human interest, they are ready to strike in when needed rather than remain aloof. Because they feel the problems of others and see their needs, they are the more ready to intervene helpfully and to take on themselves responsibilities which may bring burdens but which make life real. Perhaps this is what that particular old scholar meant.

It is hard for anyone to know what he might or might not have been had this or that influence not come his way. There are countless people who have all the good qualities we have described and it cannot be said by any means that all old scholars possess them. Waldorf education does not create these qualities but it certainly sets out to serve them. There is no doubt that the imaginative approach of the earlier years translates itself into insight and initiative later and that the reverence for man which is cultivated leads to a heightening of social responsibility. It is also true that the education sets out to foster a balance of outlook which mitigates against political and other forms of fanaticism and which upholds the purely human.

For Whom Are These Schools Intended?
Is this education specially adapted for Europeans? Is it as good for others?

This education is born of a new conception of man and is intended for man wherever he may be. It bears a world character: that is why it has spread to so many lands already and continues to spread. Before the war, the Dutch had a successful Rudolf Steiner school in Java. Outer events, unfortunately, brought it to an end.

An Indian educator, a lady, once visited a Waldorf School in England. It was explained to her that one of the endeavours of the education was to hold back a too-rapid intellectual development and instead to encourage greater force of imagination. Her comment was interesting. It appeared to her that this same education applied in India could serve in the opposite way, namely, to counter the tendency to remain too long suspended in images and to bring the intellect to birth more quickly. She thus gave tribute both to the universality and the ready adaptability of this education.

Today, through the initiative of a courageous man and his wife, Indians who had each spent a time at Emerson College and visited Waldorf Schools not only in England but in Norway, Holland, Switzerland and Germany, there are a number of nursery-kindergartens, Waldorf in type, and a school in Dalhousie. It is a pioneering work which needs and deserves all the help it can get, not least through visits of Waldorf-trained teachers to help and train further native teachers that are there.

In South America there is a Waldorf School of a thousand children at Sao Paulo in Brazil, as well as three others; there are two schools in Argentina, two in Colombia, one in Peru and in Uruguay and an initiative in Mexico.

In our intellectual West we tend to set the same kind of standard for all peoples and for all the individuals of any one people. That is why our theories fall so easily to the ground where human relationships are concerned. But man is so much more than a speculative brain. However useful and necessary the intellect may be, the forces which guide life lie much deeper. It is in these depths that man has his true being and it is out of these depths that understanding must come from man to man. Until that time comes, there will be no peace on this earth. Waldorf education wishes to serve the all-human in every man.

Examinations

It will have become clear that the type of work needed for examinations falls outside the primary aims and intentions of a Waldorf School. The examinations required for entering college or the professional schools, far from forming our culminating work, invade and compromise the curriculum of our upper classes. Where the examination pressure grows acute, there may easily arise conflict in the mind as between the immediate and so-called practical results of the examination and the ultimate and truly practical results at which this education aims. Each school, within the compass of its given possibilities, tries to arrange its programme as best it can to meet both the immediate and the ultimate ends. In general it can be said that the examination results in our schools compare well with those in other schools. Less time is spent on this work than elsewhere; on the other hand, to safeguard the Waldorf curriculum as far as possible, the examinations are generally taken later. The sacrifices involved in keeping a child that much longer at school should be weighed against the benefits of doing so spread over a whole lifetime.

Perhaps something further needs to be added, for, indeed, the question of examinations cannot be glossed over—it affects the lives of children too nearly, and their parents also. There is such a deep-rooted bias towards the intellectual. A class in which children have worked and grown in happy harmony for years suddenly, confronted with the examination problem, falls apart into those who can, those who might, and those who cannot. This is a matter of real distress and results in a totally false evaluation of human merits. There are Steiner Schools which have set up, running parallel to the examination class, a whole department in arts and crafts carried to completion of apprenticeship level, with excellent results, but still the prejudice persists that anything that falls short of the academic must somehow be inferior. Today there is many a college graduate walking about with his hands in his pockets, obliged for lack of employment to live on the dole, whilst there is a call in all trades for real craftsmen described as a dying race.

What is the examination—that is, the school leaving exam—in reality? The syllabus is fragmentary and superficial. In the examination little more is demanded than a recapitulation of prescribed facts. To the extent that some degree of thinking is called for, it is still the standard answer, pre-established in the mind of the examiner, that scores highest. Originality is neither looked for nor expected—it even becomes for the examiner a matter for embarrassment. Everything is tuned to be so-called objective. In the last resort, the Yes-No type of computerized test is the most objective of all! There, even the examiner is *de trop*, and the matters are entirely depersonalized. Yet it is the examination alone which offers the means of entry to colleges and the professions.

How different is the case with some of the older universities where the main importance attaches to a three-hour essay on a subject chosen there and then out of a given list for which there could have been no previous preparation. The subjects listed are all concerned with broad aspects of life and knowledge. Here the examiner's main interest is to discover whatever is unique in mind and expression in the young applicant. Originality of thought and imagination are actually looked for. The examiner is free to do justice to what comes to meet him irrespective of personal views and convictions. Here is a condition of what might be called *human* objectivity and true regard for culture.

The trend has gone far away from this. Yet, since action and reaction are a real part of life, there are signs of a new liberality arising here and there, reaching towards a freer and more enlightened outlook. It is not too much to say that dry and pedantic over-intellectualism is threatening to be the death of us and of nature too. It is high time to recognize that the human being is endowed with a threefold nature in thought and feeling and will, and nothing short of attention to all three will do. Therefore, a young person, if he is to be tested at all, should in justice be tested in all three: he should be given an opportunity to reveal his powers of thought, so, too, his capacity for artistic appreciation and expression, and, not least, evidence of his ability to handle a practical skill. There would then be a basis for a balanced assessment of all three faculties and how best to advise each one of his further course. This would go far to abolish the false scale of values which prevails today. We might then learn to honour head and heart and limb in equal measure, all three making up a total human being.

That is precisely what is striven for in Waldorf Schools, where the teachers unite in their endeavours to build up a truly objective picture of each child to be recognized by both the children according to their age and by their parents for their further guidance. This way no formal examinations are called for or found necessary. The nearest approach to such freedom in procuring formal recognition and the grant of a public certificate has occurred in a number of schools, notably in Germany. The teachers in these schools are able to set their own examination based on their own syllabus of requirements. They also do their own invigilating in the familiar school premises, the only proviso being that a representative of the educational authorities should be in general attendance. This is the most human situation that has offered itself so far. Such schools are truly privileged and all concerned can be grateful. Here is a situation, essentially human, based on trust.

Competition

Since, so I understand, you do not encourage competition, how are your children prepared to enter a competitive world?

Stronger than the spirit of competition is the spirit of emulation, the readiness to appreciate what is admirable in others, and therefore worthy of being striven for. Thus each is encouraged to do better. The only worthwhile competition is with oneself, to outgrow what one is in striving to become what one might be. That is the spirit above all which needs to be encouraged. It is then not a question of whether or not one is better than another but whether one is oneself at one's best. Emulation becomes a far-reaching force in life, a moral and redeeming force, whereas competition has no mercy for the weaker and breeds egotism.

A teacher has endless opportunities to draw the attention of his children to the happy use of a word, a phrase, or an image in someone's composition, or maybe a striking use of colour, or a commendable point of behaviour—*something* to be justly extolled now in the one child, now in another. In an exhibition of class work no one is ever left out, and so it is in daily life. There is also the case of a child who is known to have had a difficulty, and who then, by dint of great effort, is able to surmount it. That is a matter of rejoicing for the whole class. That is what difficulties are for, to be surmounted, and thereby we grow.

Emulation encourages charity of heart, something much needed at all times, and leads to a future society born in fellowship. Competition, as can be seen all too easily in our 'competitive world', hardens people into an attitude of each for himself before all else. One is led to believe that conquest is through force, but such conquest always fails. One can also conquer through the gift of love which is ready to make room for another. Such conquest has in it something that abides.

There is no point in moralizing in these matters but of only recognizing the truth. The educator, if he is true to his task, is concerned with that 'greater strength' in man which outvies the competitive. It is, after all, ideals we have to serve, and one so easily falls into the error of seeing the ideal as something weak in the face of the so-called real. The prophets, we are told, have ever been persecuted, but it is they that survive. Where should we be without them?

Chapter 9

TO PARENTS

Parents will have their own reasons for choosing to send their children to a private school. No doubt they will have made careful enquiry into the character of the school and the particular benefits it offers. That this should be the case in connection with Waldorf Schools is highly desirable, for the life of these schools depends to a great degree on close understanding and co-operation between parents and teachers. It needs to be understood that what is offered in these schools is not the product of just another educational theory but is based on a total view of life that touches religion, art, science, history, reaching into the very heart of what we might come to see as the real grounds of knowledge and of life on earth. Rudolf Steiner himself said that the Waldorf Schools would grow because they were seen to be good schools, that is, schools that do good to children. That was the basis on which Michael Hall received official recognition. The inspectors did not feel they needed to enter into the philosophy of the school— they judged by what they saw to be its fruits, and to a large extent that is the case with many of the parents. Yet there are always some who want to pursue things further. The question has been asked, for example, whether, since all the teachers serve a common ideal, there might not be some danger of indoctrination.

Once we have come to acknowledge the fact that education down to the most elementary levels is dominated by tenets of materialistic science, we may also readily see that we are already indoctrinated from the start by a one-sided view of man and the world; moreover one that undermines human values and is leading to wholesale havoc in public and in private life. The very triumphs of our advancing technology have multiplied disaster and have overwhelmed humanity with threats and anxieties on a fearsome scale. Waldorf teachers take fully into account the positive achievements of our time, but they also perceive the moral as well as the material dangers that are invading life. They strive to develop a view both of nature and of human nature which includes the moral with the physical, correcting the one-sidedness of materialism. Then man, instead of being a mere onlooker of a world which, as is supposed, could go on just as well without him, becomes an integral part of the whole of creation bringing new meanings to all that comes to meet him. It becomes natural, as Rudolf Steiner proposed, that man should hold a central place in every subject taught. What the school is doing is, far from indoctrinating, to provide a corrective to the severe indoctrination which is already taking place, influencing every moment of our lives, and determining the future in which our children must play their part. It is a blessed thing for children and for the work if parents and children can enter into a mutual understanding of this.

Let us carry this somewhat further. The world is presented as being ruled by number. The eighteenth century view that mathematics is the key to the universe still in the main prevails. Let us take the simple example of a piano. The construction is most certainly ruled by number, but insofar as the piano is an instrument for music, the numbers are subject to the indefinable laws and realities of the art of music. It calls for the skilled musician to reveal what the piano is actually meant to be. Slowly, very slowly as yet, such a view is beginning to dawn for the whole of creation. Number is there, and construction is there in mineral, plant, animal, man, in physics, chemistry and all the sciences, number in the proportions to be met in art as well as nature, number in all the rhythms that permeate all nature, above all, living nature—number is there not as the *cause* but as the revealed *consequence* of what rules in creation. Our science has arrived at a quantitative view of the world in which quality, beauty in nature and morality in man become uneasy presences. This way the world is viewed as a machine and man as an inconsequent cipher. Clearly if this view is to persist, it can only bring ruination in its wake. We have to find a way, a *scientific* way of arriving at the perception of the world as a meaningful work of art, and of man as the bearer of a new evolving morality, in his unceasing striving for truth, beauty, wisdom, love.

In this endeavour, born of the life-long work of Rudolf Steiner, a Waldorf School, if rightly understood, stands in the forefront of genuine progress towards a saner future. The work is bound to prosper to the extent that parents, out of their own life experience, come to see the truth of this. Then any fear of indoctrination must simply fall away, and the work be seen as one that is intended to help free human faculties from their present bondage to matter.

Our older children are not unaware of the fact that in many respects they are being taught differently. We record an occasion when a group of sixteen-year-olds, who had been brought up mainly in a Waldorf School, approached a teacher with the following direct questions.

'We would like to know what you have been teaching us. For example, you have often spoken to us of the threefold man. We would like to know whether what you have been teaching us is what you think, or what Dr. Steiner thinks, or what the world thinks.' The teacher answered somewhat as follows: 'What I have taught you is what I think, but in arriving at the thoughts I have shared with you I was very much helped by the thoughts of Rudolf Steiner. It is not the way the world in general thinks today. But of this I can fully assure you. You will have no difficulty in understanding what will be brought to you at College of the way the world thinks, but you may recall that there is another possible approach to the same phenomena.

Now who will be in a better position to form a free judgement, he who has met only the one dominant view, as expressed in the textbooks, or someone who will be in a position to compare this with at least one other point of view?'

There was a pause, and then one of the young company, a choleric, thumped his chest and said, 'Mr.X. I declare myself thoroughly satisfied.'

Many years later most of that group met the same teacher again. This same student, now well established in his profession, now asked: 'Are you not disappointed, Mr. X., that so few of us have followed your point of view?'

And Mr. X. replied, 'No, I am not disappointed. My object was not that you should follow my point of view, but that you should be better able to arrive at your own point of view.'

Looking back over the years, the young people of the first interview, now entering middle age, could agree that far from being subjected to dogma or being indoctrinated, they had been prepared for a life of inner freedom in which they could find themselves.

One cannot be long acquainted with a Waldorf School without hearing of Rudolf Steiner and his teaching which he called Anthroposophy. People find it a puzzling word. It actually combines two words, *anthropos*, man, as in anthropology, and *sophia*, wisdom, as in philosophy, *man-wisdom*. Man, we will admit, is still the greatest mystery we can meet on earth, and wisdom we know to be something other than knowledge. A wise man is one who has insight, one who can see life from within. A fuller interpretation of the word anthroposophy might be spiritual insight into the world as revealed through the nature of man. An American professor once wrote: In these days of exploration of outer space is it not necessary that we also begin an exploration of inner space? That is precisely what Anthroposophy sets out to do, but whereas from outer space man makes use of many outer instruments, for inner space he himself must become the instrument, that is, he has to develop further the faculties with which he finds himself already endowed, namely, his thinking, feeling and willing. There are words in common usage which point in the direction of such a development. We say of someone he has a powerful imagination; of another that he is greatly inspired; of a third that he is profound in his intuitions. All three words, imagination, inspiration, intuition, carry the mind beyond the everyday. Anthroposophy offers disciplines whereby any one who has the will can develop these faculties, possessed by all human beings in varying degree, into higher organs of perception. In the past we have lived very much by the gifts of the chosen few. Today, it behoves each one, as a modern human being, to strive in a measure to join their ranks, if only to justify his claim to take full responsibility for his outer life.

That is what the teacher meant who said to that group of children that he teaches as *he* thinks, not as he has been told to think, even though he admits his great indebtedness to Rudolf Steiner. The age of authority in the old sense has gone. It is because human beings do not sufficiently realize this and therefore fail to find the authority within themselves that the world is largely falling subject to all manner of outer controls, so that one begins to wonder whether the dreamed-of age of human freedom will ever come. Our romantic poets thought the French revolution had opened the way to it with the cry, 'Liberty, Equality, Fraternity,' but they were sorely disappointed.

They had to learn that freedom has to come from within and that it is inseparable from the power of love. Thus Coleridge, still young, aged only twenty-five, could write:

> ....on that sea-cliff's verge,
> Whose pines, scarce travelled by the breeze above,
> Had made one murmur with the distant surge!
> Yes, while I stood and gazed, my temples bare,
> And shot my being through earth, sea, and air,
> Possessing all things with intensest love,
> O Liberty! my spirit felt thee there.

Do we teach Anthroposophy? No, we do not, but we try to teach in such a way that it may lead towards the fullness of an experience such as that of Coleridge—that it may open ways, within the grasp of each one, to advance his inner life, and therefore also outer life, further. To help towards this is possible through education. Parents can surely help towards this. The first years of a child's life, before even kindergarten begins, are entirely in their hands. This goes right back to the moment of birth and even earlier. At a meeting with young and expectant mothers the picture was brought up of the Annuciation by the Archangel Gabriel to Mary in the Gospel of St. Luke. There is that wonderful moment of the first realization that *a child is on the way*. Surely every child that comes into this world must have a similar annunciation! And then so very much depends on the environment created, first the love that streams to the child; but an informed love that also knows how to attend to outer conditions, the right degree of light, of warmth, the right colours on the walls for the very young child; the right diet when the time comes (our doctors advise against meat in the early years); the right regularity of habits, the waking to the day with a song and a prayer, and even more so at the settling down to sleep; and the right toys, simple, colourful, *not* mechanical, not porcelain dolls that shut their eyes, and so on. These first years are the most deeply impressionable in the whole of life. The child, says Rudolf Steiner, is one great sense organ, it absorbs every impression around it. Young parents need to study these things and, if need be, seek help and advice.

Then, when the child goes to the Nursery or Kindergarten, parents again can observe, consult, bring the home life into harmony with what the child receives at school. What shall the child best wear as the year goes round, especially in the winter to protect its body warmth?

And then come the eight years with the class teacher—one great continuous adventure. It is above all important that parents should not merely accept what the school does and gives but they should *know why* reading is introduced later, feeling assured of the rightness of this—the why and the when and the how of everything done; the parents have a right to know, and the teachers will be happy to share, to consult and be consulted. Childhood is not merely a succession of years, each year is different and there are also *crisis years*, times of special change which need to be well understood.

And then come the high school years. It is not only that the children enter high school having left their class teacher. Puberty brings problems, and adolescence demands a change of relationship with parents as well as with teachers and the adult world generally. These are real changes, and the fact that certain of them tend today to come earlier calls for further study and understanding to be shared by parents and teachers, and more and more with the children also. It is a fact that a Waldorf School provides a learning and growing situation not only for the children but for the parents and teachers as well.

There are, of course, many ways in which parents can enter more closely into the social and cultural life of a Waldorf School, opportunities not only to study but to be introduced also to the arts, maybe to eurythmy, to painting, to music. Then there are festival occasions and exhibition times when parents can have a survey not only of their own children's classes but of the whole school. There is generally a parent-teacher association. There is a great need for pioneer parents as well as pioneer teachers to carry the whole Waldorf Movement further into the world, so that the benefits of this education may reach the greatest number of children possible. We need parents also who can grow articulate about the education in meeting others.

A lot of work for all, but we hope a joyous work!

Chapter 10

THE FORM AND ORGANIZATION
OF A WALDORF SCHOOL

A Rudolf Steiner or Waldorf School is co-educational throughout. It is not merely that boys and girls are taught together and that men and women share the work alike. The aim is so to educate through Art that it may bring new life to Science and so to educate through Science that it may bring greater consciousness to Art. True co-education consists in establishing the right relationship between these two, between feeling penetrated with thought and thought permeated with feeling, and for this it is most fitting to have the sexes grow up side by side. In the past, the ideal of the man was to be outstandingly male, the ideal of the woman to be completely female. In the individualized society of today this is no longer so. The male needs to acquire some of the qualities which in the female yield plasticity of soul, the female needs equally to gain those qualities which in the male lead to greater clarity and independence of thought. It has become a commonplace to talk of the equality of the sexes. This does not deny the reality of sex values but points rather to a society of the future which will rest more and more upon those intrinsic human qualities which reach beyond male and female. Signs of this are to be seen everywhere. The relationship between men and women in public life is very different from what it was fifty years ago. That this change can best be served by co-education only the diehard few of yesterday will care to question.

Waldorf Schools take children right through from the age of three or four to eighteen or nineteen, for childhood is viewed as a progressive whole, though with well-defined phases as described previously. So connected are the three great periods of childhood that to cut through them wilfully is like cutting into life itself. It is good for older children to recall their own earlier years in the younger children round them and good for the younger children to glimpse something of the years which lie ahead as they look towards the older children. One of the most interesting and impressive innovations in a Waldorf School is the monthly or termly Children's Festival. Children up and down the school present examples to the rest of the school of work they have done in class, recitation in their mother tongue and in foreign languages, flute playing, singing, a play they have prepared, a scene out of the history lessons, a demonstration from the science class, a piece of eurythmy or some of their gymnastic exercises, and so on. It is at such a Festival that the corporate unity of the school is experienced powerfully. As for the teachers, their continued association in work which covers the whole range of these years educates an accurate insight into childhood life and growth as nothing else can.

A Waldorf School takes its form from the fact that all three periods of childhood are included. The very little children, before they enter the school proper, form a self-contained community in themselves. Then comes the succession of eight classes, each with its own Class Teacher. These classes are referred to by the name of the Class Teacher and only rarely by number. Finally, there is the upper school with its circle of Specialist Teachers. The same plan holds good for the larger schools with their parallel classes.

There are no prefects with badges and no set appointments. The feeling of seniority comes from the changing relationship with the teachers and amongst the students themselves and particularly from the work in the classroom, the problems discussed, the tasks which are given and the demands made. The exercise of leadership is not overlooked, but instead of having a system with fixed appointments it is called upon as actual needs and situations arise. Since these are bound to vary, different children have opportunities given them to serve in different ways according to their gifts and capacities. In this way life is kept at a continuous flow. As given demands arise, the capacity to meet them springs into place; there is no rigid pattern. Some question this until they see its greater virtue. They would prefer formal appointments, rules, rewards and punishments. This evades the problem of self-discipline; yet command over self, not command over others, is the first prerequisite of any free society. Genuine authority cannot be taught, it has to be engendered. Therefore, contrary to the methods of self-government practised in other schools, in a Waldorf School final authority rests solely with the adults, though consultative meetings between teachers and the older scholars have now become customary—indeed they are seen to be essential for the happy conduct of a high school.

In a Waldorf School there is not the same need as elsewhere for a headmaster. The Nursery Class teacher represents the school to the parents of the children in her care. Each class teacher quite obviously takes first responsibility for his class and is best suited to deal with the parents of his children. Each specialist teacher is similarly responsible for his department; they work things out together. Upper school parents may consult whom they will, though, for routine purposes, it has been found useful for each upper school class to have one teacher as a class adviser or counsellor. All the teachers with their different spheres of responsibility meet together as a body, and it is this collective body which has the final direction of the school. The body of teachers, often referred to as College of Teachers (really the Colleagueship of Teachers), appoints its own chairman, executive, and whatever other functionaries may be needed. Such appointments are more in the nature of delegations taking account of the special gifts and capacities which the one or other may have to serve the whole. The personnel engaged changes from time to time. This method of delegation makes for continuity in the work and yet for greater freedom for the teachers. A teacher will undertake the task that it seems best for him to undertake at a given time. At another time he may be able to serve best in another way. On the other hand, the character of the school need never depend on any one individual or group of individuals; the essential character will be maintained by the directing body of teachers even if, in course of time, the individuals comprising that body should totally change.

The teacher body carries all ultimate responsibility for the school but it generally has an advisory body of governors or trustees and an administrative office staff.

Finally it should be added that Waldorf Schools are independent entities, each responsible for itself and its own maintenance. There is friendly co-operation between schools but no central organization to rule over them. The only ruling principle is the work which is common to them all, the uniting factor being the study of the child in the light of Rudolf Steiner's deep wisdom as has been briefly outlined in these pages.

Chapter 11

THE RANGE OF RUDOLF STEINER'S WORK FOR CHILDREN

Rudolf Steiner education has also become associated with handicapped children. The work for these children has developed magnificently since its first inception, some few years after the founding of the original Waldorf School in 1919; its very success has led to certain misconceptions which it is our purpose here to correct.

It was Rudolf Steiner's view that schools founded on his methods should gain ground simply through their recognition as *good schools*. Their progress has been of this kind. It was quickly found, however, that the methods used were of great benefit to many children who were otherwise in difficulties. Very soon, children began to come recommended by doctors, psychologists, child guidance clinics and educational authorities; grateful parents spread their good news further and all this gave rise to the idea that these schools could deal with special cases—nay, indeed, that they were in some way special schools. Thus, what was good news in the first place turned to error. The question of the 'problem' child is a widespread and harassing one. A lecture on the handicapped, the maladjusted or the delinquent child will always draw large audiences. In point of fact our schools have to be extremely circumspect not to be besieged with requests for children.

It next happened that Rudolf Steiner was approached from several quarters for advice about badly retarded and sick children, including such familiar types as mongols, epileptics, hysterics, spastics, hydrocephalics, schizophrenics and others. As a result *homes* for such children began to spring up, notably in Germany, Switzerland, Holland and England (later in Scotland also). Men and women came forward with great and noble zeal to throw themselves heart and soul into this work, and their attitude to these children, inspired by Rudolf Steiner's teaching, become something very new. The children were regarded not merely as 'unfortunates' but, out of deepened understanding of human destiny, as sufferers for the human race, bearers of the widespread ills of mankind focused on themselves. Far from being mere recipients, they were looked upon as bringers of a moral challenge to our times: the intellect can serve them little—quite other forces, the most deeply human of which we are capable, are called into action for, in the case of such children, treatment not born of profound devotion and love is of little avail. This work, also carried on in the name of Rudolf Steiner, has grown splendidly, with great sacrifice, and is constantly discovering new ways and means; in it the ideals described in these pages are led down to the most needy and sick. Such centres may well be called 'homes', for these seemingly helpless ones have no *home* elsewhere on this earth, and in these homes where they are met with spiritual understanding their happiness is marvellous to behold.

Mention may here be made of the Camphill Movement founded by the late Dr. Karl Koenig and now grown to become a world movement in its own right. It comprises 'The Camphill Rudolf Steiner Schools for Children in Need of Special Care', training facilities for work with such children, and also a number of Camphill Villages, run as working community centres for mentally handicaped young people and adults.

It became apparent that there was a wide range of children not catered for either by the Waldorf Schools for normal children, or by the Rudolf Steiner Schools and Homes for the mentally retarded. Such children were loosely described as 'maladjusted'—that might mean emotionally disturbed, or delinquent, or generally undernourished and underdeveloped in their mental, moral and social being. Perhaps the most dangerous were those with the highest mental grades. Their troubles were generally referred back to the lack of love they received in their infancy and early childhood but could also be due to over-pampering. One way or another they could be regarded as the direct victims of maladjusted society. They, too, needed the utmost 'special care', educational, medical, social and environmental, to bring them into better harmony in themselves and with their fellows, and, when older, a training in some craft to help them find their way into the main stream of life. A number of Rudolf Steiner Centres have come into being, mostly in Great Britain, generally described as 'Home-Schools' to deal with these particular needs. The work they do is truly of a rehabilitation character with wide implications and possibilities.

We may see how the name of Rudolf Steiner has become associated with every imaginable type and condition of childhood. In this he stands unique for all time in the field of education. He died in 1925 but the work he began continues to grow, expand and find ever new ground. There are, today, over six hundred Waldorf Schools in the world, even more children's Homes, as well as the 'Home-Schools'. All these find their underlying support in the basic conceptions of child development with which these pages are concerned. If this be understood, then there need be no confusion in regard to the specific tasks of the work with *normal* children as well as with the different types of *disturbed* children.

Chapter 12

THE WALDORF SCHOOL MOVEMENT

Waldorf education dates back to September, 1919, with the founding of the first Waldorf School by Rudolf Steiner himself. This took place in Stuttgart in Southern Germany at the request of the then director of the Waldorf Astoria Cigarette Company in that city. It was designed in the first place for the children of the factory employees, thus springing into being directly out of modern industrial life. The school grew leaps and bounds to the size of a thousand children drawing its pupils from many parts of Germany, from other countries in Europe and even from as far away as America. In the years that followed ten other schools were founded in Germany and schools arose also. Hitler openly declared that the philosophy in these schools with its emphasis on nurturing individuality ran contrary to that of National Socialism, and therefore they must close. That left during the war years some half a dozen small struggling schools as between Switzerland, England, and North America. There was little or no communication betwen them and the outlook was extremely bleak.

Immediately after the war ended, the schools began to revive, to grow, and to multiply almost too quickly for the lack of teachers trained in the Waldorf methods. There are schools today in England, Scotland and Ireland in Great Britain, in Norway, Sweden, Finland, Denmark, Holland, Belgium, France, Germany, Austria, Italy, USA, Canada, Australia, New Zealand, South Africa, Brazil, Argentina, and early beginnings in India. This distribution of schools has come about through no kind of central plan or directive. On the contrary, each school is an entirely independent enterprise, resting wholly on the initiatives of teachers and parents and whatever local support they may find. It is in this way alone that there has come about a Waldorf World Movement, purely on the merits of the work itself and what it offers. Every such school entails great sacrifice on the part of the teachers, parents and friends. Nevertheless the work continues to grow, more easily in those countries, notably Denmark, Germany, Norway, and to some extent Holland and Finland in Europe, and also Australia and New Zealand, where the governments do in a measure subsidize private education. This, unhappily, is not the case in Britain, Canada, the United States, and the other countries mentioned. Yet there are now twenty-six schools in Great Britain and more to be opened; there are over seventy schools in the United States and thirteen in Canada; there are six in South Africa, seventeen in Australia and four in New Zealand. In a small country like Holland there are over eighty and Germany has nearly one hundred and thirty.

So much for the outer facts. It remains to be asked, what is the driving force behind this movement? This, it is hoped, will have become apparent through the description of the education given. The basic outline for such a form of education was given by Rudolf Steiner as far back as 1907, but the first direct request for a school did not come until human conscience had been stirred to the uttermost by the fearful calamity of the First World War. This left all thinking people stunned with a sense of moral and social failure and the collapse of all the alluring hopes men had been nursing for an era just ahead of assured peace, industrial progress and economic security on an ever widening scale. The phase that followed that war period was one of large scale dictatorships which, in turn, led directly into the Second World War. Today we are floundering in a morass of doubts and uncertainties with new horrors assailing the headlines every day. All this gives evidence of a fact that few can fail to recognize, namely that we find ourselves entangled in the decaying elements of an old world order with its traditional faiths and authorities and that the world awaits the birth of a new faith, a new vision, and a new conscience, a new awakening to the reality of man as a spiritual being, suffering through finding himself divorced from his own true being. How can he rediscover himself and, in so doing, find that despite all the frantic contradictions of the time, the sustaining forces of all existence are still the realities of truth, beauty, goodness which find their fulfilment in love? It is out of renewed knowledge of man, a knowledge imbued with wisdom, (Anthropos-Sophia) that Waldorf education has been born. Waldorf education directs itself to the growing forces of the child, to the ground of human morality perceived in the healthy life of play of the infant years, to the ground of social being expressed in the healthy life of feeling in the childhood years, to the ground of mutual understanding based on a healthy enhancement of thinking in the adolescent years, so that the young adult, when he comes to himself, may find himself at home in the world. Since these are actual needs and not inventions, more and more people are learning to recognize in Waldorf education a means to enable children, through the right engaging of their faculties in the ordered sequence of the years, to grow into a generation of men and women with more likely answers to the world situation than are possessed today. Truly the future must lie with the maturing forces of childhood which carry within themselves the mystery of man's becoming. The task of education is to nurture these forces so that they may find their truest possible expression in the years to come in individual and public life.

Chapter 13

WALDORF TEACHER TRAINING

A question often asked is, 'How do you find your teachers?' The most obvious answer is, 'Life brings them'. The teachers we meet in the Waldorf Schools are men and women who found their way to them in the course of their search for enlightened human values and out of a deep concern for the social future. Some were teachers already before they heard of Waldorf Schools and Rudolf Steiner. Others, finding Anthroposophy, were led on to become teachers. There are several centres today which offer special training in Waldorf methods. In broad terms the following are the elements of training common to them all:

A study of man in his threefold nature of body, soul and spirit.

A detailed study of child development in all its phases including a particular study of the temperaments.

The Waldorf Curriculum in its intimate relationship to the forces of growing childhood in infancy, the elementary school years and adolescence. (It is required that all teachers should acquire an overall view to which they can then best relate their particular contributions).

Story telling and story making, also for remedial purposes.

Tutorial Courses in basic subjects such as mathematics, literature, history, history of art, music, the sciences, etc.

Continued practice in the arts: weekly classes in speech and eurythmy and block periods in painting and modelling; also optional classes in recorder playing, crafts and, where this can be provided, in Bothmer gymnastics.

Classroom observation and practice teaching.

Organizational aspects, parent-teacher relationship, medical questions, etc.

The following are the best known and the longest established of the Waldorf Teacher Training Centres, though as the Waldorf Movement continues to grow and expand new centres are opening up. No given list can be up-to-date for very long but further information is always available on enquiry. At most of these centres there is a preliminary year of study and artistic work, comparable to the Foundation Year at Emerson College, before procedure to the educational studies proper.

In England
Emerson College, Forest Row, Sussex, RH18 5JX.

In the U.S.A.
Rudolf Steiner College, 9200 Fair Oaks Boulevard,
Fair Oaks, CA. 95628.

Waldorf Institute of S. California, 17100 Superior Street
Northridge CA 91325.

Waldorf Institute, 260 Hungry Hollow Road,
Spring Valley, New York 10977.

Antioch University, Antioch/New England Graduate School,
Roxbury Street, Keene, New Hampshire 03431.

In Switzerland
Lehrerseminar, Brosiweg 5, CH 4143 Dornach.

In Germany
Seminar für Waldorfpädagogik, Haussmannstrasse 44A, D-7000
Stuttgart 1.

Institut für Waldorfpädagogik, Annener Berg 15,
D-5810 Witten-Annen.

Freie Hochschule für anthroposophische Pädagogik, Zielstrasse
28, D-6800 Mannheim 1.

Lehrerseminar für Waldorfpädagogik, Brabantestrasse 43,
D-3500 Kassel-Wilhelmshöhe.

There are also seminars in Hamburg, Heidenheim, Kiel and
Nuremberg.

In Sweden
Rudolf Steiner Seminariet, S-15300 Järna.

Kirstofferseminariet, Box 124, S-16126 Bromma.

In France
Perceval Pédagogie Rudolf Steiner, 5 rue Georges-Clemenceau, F-78400 Chatou.

In the Netherlands
Vrije Pedagogische Akademie, Socrateslaan 22A, NL-3707 GL Zeist.

There are also full time courses in Australia, Austria, Canada, Denmark, Finland, New Zealand, Norway, South Africa and South America.

Information on the many part-time and in-training courses are available through the national Waldorf School organizations. (In Great Britain this is: The Steiner Schools' Fellowship, Kidbrooke Mansion, Michael Hall, Forest Row, E. Sussex RH18 5JB. Tel: 034282 2115.)

WALDORF (RUDOLF STEINER) SCHOOLS

A number of schools have developed a system of in-service training.
Please enquire.

ARGENTINA
Buenos Aires Colegio Incorporado "Paula Albarracin de Sarmiento" — Rudolf Steiner-Schule Warnes 1357, 1602 Pcia de Buenos Aires.
Buenos Aires Escuela San Miguel Arcángel, José Maria Moreno 1221, 1607 Villa Adelina, Buenos Aires.

AUSTRALIA
Association of Rudolf Steiner Schools in Australia, Box 82, P.O., Round Corner, Dural. 2158. Participants in Association.
Bangalow Cape Byron Rudolf Steiner School, P.O. Box 41, Bangalow, N.S.W. 2479.
Bowral Eukarima School, Centennial Road, Bowral, N.S.W. 2576.
Cawongla Daystar Rudolf Steiner School, R.M.B. Cawongla via Kyogle 2574.
Dorrigo Plateau Steiner School, 77 Myrtle Street, Dorrigo 2453.
Hazelbrook Blue Mountains Waldorf School, 77 Clearview Parade, Hazelbrook.
Maitland Linuwel School for Rudolf Steiner Education, 133 Morpeth Road, East Maitland, N.S.W. 2323.
Manuka Orana School for Rudolf Steiner Education, P.O. Box 492, Manuka Act 2603.
Melbourne Melbourne Rudolf Steiner School, 213 Wonga Road, Warranwood, Vic. 3134.
Mount Barker Waldorf School for Rudolf Steiner Education, Sims Road, Mount Barker S.A. 5251.
Nedlands The Waldorf School for Rudolf Steiner Education, P.O. Box 291, Nedlands W.A. 6009.
Newcastle Newcastle Rudolf Steiner School, 35 Reservoir Road, Glendale 2285.
Perth Perth Waldorf School, P.O. Box 49 Hamilton Hill, W.A. 6163.
Sydney Glenaeon School, 5a Glenroy Ave., Middle Cove, N.S.W. 2068.
Sydney Lorien Novalis School for Rudolf Steiner Education Ltd., 456 Old Northern Road, Dural, N.S.W. 2158.
Sydney Lorien Novalis College of Teacher Education, address as above.
Thora Chrysalis School for Rudolf Steiner Education, Darkwood Road, Thora, N.S.W. 2492.
Victoria/Yarra Little Yarra Steiner School, P.O. Box 19, Yarra Junction 3797, Victoria.
Yarramundi Aurora-Meander School for Rudolf Steiner Education, Lot 1 Mountain Ave., Yarramundi, N.S.W. 2753.

AUSTRIA
Graz Freie Waldorfschule, St. Peter Hauptstraße 182,, A 8042 Graz.
Innsbruck Freie Waldorschule Innsbruck, Jahnstraße 5, A 6020 Innsbruck.
Klagenfurt Rudolf-Steiner-Schule Klagenfurt, Wilsonstraße 11, A 9020 Klagenfurt.
Linz Freie Waldorfschule, Baumbachstraße 11, A 4020 Linz.
Salzburg Rudolf-Steiner-Schule, Bayerhamerstraße 35, A 5020 Salzburg.
Wien-Mauer Rudolf-Steiner-Schule, Endresstraße 100, A 1238 Wien 23.
Wien-Pötzleinsdorf Rudolf-Steiner-Schule, Geymüllergaße 1, A 1180 Wien.

BELGIUM
Aalst Michaeli, Hertshage 39, 9300 Aalst.
Antwerpen De Hazelaar, Lange Lozannastraat 117, 2018 Antwerpen.
Antwerpen Rudolf Steinerschool, Prins Albertlei 19, 2600 Berchem.
Antwerpen Hibernia, Rodestraat 23, 2000 Antwerpen.
Brasschaat De Wingerd, Zwemdoklei 3, 2130 Brasschaat.
Brugge Guido Gezellschool, Bilkske 5, 8000, Brugge.
Bruxelles Ecole Rudolf Steiner, Rue Willemijns 335A, 1070 Anderlecht, Bruxelles.
Erembodegem Michaelischool, Brusselbaan 300, 9440 Erembodegem.
Eupen Rudolf Steinerschule Eupen, p.a. Walter Hammacker, Forsthaus Mospert, Schönfeld 241, 4700 Eupen.
Gent Vrije Rudolf Steiner School, Kasteelaan 54, 9000 Gent.
Leuven De Zonnewijzer, Weldadigheidstraat 74, 3000, Leuven.
Lier De Sterredaalders, Mallekotstraat 41, 2500 Lier.
Overijse Kristoffelschool, Mollenburg 7, 1900 Overijse.
Turnhout Michaëlschool, Steenweg op Oosthoven 27a, 2300 Turnhout.
Wilrijk/Antwerpen Rudolf Steinerschool, Lohangrin Boomse Steenweg 94, 2610 Wilrijk.

BRAZIL
Sao Paulo Escola Rudolf Steiner de Sao Paulo, Rue Sao Benedito, 1325, casa 45, CEP 04735 Sao Paulo, Caixa Postal 55051-CEP 04799.
Sao Paulo Colégio Micael, Rua Pedro Alexandrino Soares 68, Jardin Boa Vista (Butantâ), 05584 Sao Paulo/Brasil.
Botcatu Aitiara-Escola do Campo, Estancia Demetria, Caxia Postal 102, 18600 Botucatu S.P.
Florianopolis Associacao Pedogogica Micael, Rua Rosato Evangelista 65, 88085 Itaguacu-Florianopolis S.C.

CANADA
* *Member of Association of Waldorf Schools of North America.*
ALBERTA
Calgary Calgary Waldorf School K-6, 1915-36th Ave. S.W., Calgary, AB T2T 2G6.
Edmonton Aurora Rudolf Steiner School, 6931-85th Street, Edmonton, AB T6C 3AE.
BRITISH COLUMBIA
Duncan Sunrise School, K-7, R.R.2, Duncan, B.C. V9L 1N9.
Kelowna Waldorf School, K-6, Box 93, 429 Collett Road, Okanagan Mission, B.C. V0H 1S0.
Nelson Nelson Waldorf School K-8, Box 165, Nelson, B.C. V1L 5P9.
* **Vancouver** Vancouver Waldorf School K-12, 2725 St. Christophers Road, North Vancouver, B.C. V7K 2B6.
Victoria Victoria Waldorf School, 1216 Oxford Street, Victoria, B.C. V8V 2V5.
ONTARIO
Cambellville Halton Waldorf School, K-6, 83 Cambellville Road East, P.O. Box 184, Cambellville, ONT, L0P 1B0.
Kitchener/Waterloo Waldorf Education Interest Group. Contact: Donna Huston 519-884 3192, Kitchener/Waterloo.
London, Ont. London Waldorf School K-8, 1697 Trafalgar Street, London, Ontario N5W 1X2.

Ottawa Ottawa Waldorf School K-8, 290 Nepean Street, Ottawa, Ontario, K1R 5G3.
* **Toronto** Toronto Waldorf School K-12, 9100 Bathurst Street, Box 220 Thornhill, Ontario L3T 3N3.
Toronto Alan Howard Waldorf School, 228 St. George Street, Toronto, Ontario, M5R 2N9.
QUEBEC
Montreal Ecole Rudolf Steiner de Montreal, K-8, 12050 Avenue de Bois de Boulogne, Montreal, P.Q. H2M 2X9.

CHILE
Santiago Colegio Rudolf Steiner, Jose Tomas Rider 1654 Providencia, Santiago-Chile.
Santiago Colegio Giordano Bruno un Colegio Waldorf, Casilla 22-11, Nunoa, Santiago-Chile.

COLUMBIA
Cali Colegio 'Luis Horàcio Gómez', Carrerra 55 No. 11-19 Barrio Santa Anita, Cali.
Medelin Colegio Isolda Echavarria, Robledo-Pilarica, Trasv. 75, 73-40, Medelin.

DENMARK
Ålborg Rudolf Steiner Skolen, Tenhojvej 14, 9220 Ålborg.
Åarhus Rudolf Steiner-Skolen i Åarhus Strand-vejen 102, 8000 Åarhus C.
Åarhus Rudolf Steiner-Vestkolen, Helm-strupgårdvej 32, 8210 Åarhus, V.
Allerıd Rudolf Steiner Skolen i Allerıd, Lyngvej 202, 3450 Allerıd.
Copenhagen Rudolf Steiner-Skolen i Hjortespring, Stokholtbuen 26, 2730 Herlev.
Copenhagen Vidar Skolen Brogaardsvej 61, 2820 Gentofte.
Fredericia Rudolf Steiner-Skolen, Kolding Landevej 7, 7000 Fredericia.
Hjırring Rudolf Steiner Skolen, Vester Thirupvej 30, 9600 Hjırring.
Kvistgård Rudolf Steiner Skolen, Kvistgård Stationvej 2A-B, 3490 Kvitsgård.
Merlıse Rudolf Steiner Skolen, Bagmarken 58, 4370 St. Merlıse.
Odense Rudolf Steiner-Skolen i Odense, Lindvedvej 64, 5260 Odense.
Odense Rudolf Steiner Skolen på Blankestedgård, Blankestedgårdvej 133, 5220 Odense SO.
Risskov Rudolf-Steiner Skolen i Vejlby-Risskov Skejbyvej 1, 8240 Risskov.
Silkeborg Rudolf Steiner-Skolen, Stanvangervej 3, 8600 Silkeborg.
Skanderborg Rudolf Steiner-Skolen Skanderborg, Grınnedalsvej 10, 8660 Skanderborg.
Vejle Johannesskolen, Rudolf Steiner-Skolen i Vejle, Sukkertoppen 4 7100 Vejle.
Vordingborg Rudolf Steiner-Skolen, Orevej 2, 4760 Vordingborg.

ECUADOR
Quito Jardin y Escuela Particular Waldorf, Gral. Perrier 695 e Jberia, Vicentina, Quito.

FINLAND
Förengen för Steinerpedagogik ry, Lehtikuusentie 6 Lärkträdsvägen, SF-00270 Helsinki 27.
Helsinki Helsingin Rudolf Steiner koulu-Rudolf Steiner skolan i Helsingfors, Lehtikuusentie 6 Lärkträdsvägen, SF-00270 Helsinki/Helsingfors 27.
Helsinki Elias-Koulu, Helsingin seuden uusi Steiner-koulu, Paraistentie 3, 00280 Helsinki.
Jyväskylä Jyväskylän Rudolf Steiner-koulu, Piilukko 33, 40630 Jyväskylä.
Karjalohja Karjalohjan vapaa kyläkoulou, Lohilampi, 09220 Sammatti.
Lahti Lahden Rudolf Steiner-koulu, Toivontie 3, 15900 Lahti 90.

Lapeenranran Lapeenranran Steinerkoulu, Tapavainola, 53850 Lapeenranran.
Oulu Oulun Sedudun Steiner-koulu, Kauppaseurrantie, 90520 Oulu.
Pori Porin Seudun Steinerkoulu, Valajankatu 2, 28100 Pori.
Rovaniemi Rovaniemen Rudolf Steiner-koulu, Lähteenie 16, 96400 Rovaniemi.
Tampere Tamperen Rudolf Steiner-koulu, Satakunnankatu 13, SF-33100 Tampere 10.
Turku Turkun Rudolf Steiner-koulu, Mestarinkatu 2, SF-20810 Turku 81.
Vaasa Vaasan Rudolf Steiner-koulu, Ravikatu 9, 65140 Vaasa.
Vantaa Vantaan Rudolf Steiner-koulu, Satakielentie 5, 01450 Vantaa 37.

FRANCE
Chatou near Paris Ecole Perceval, 5 Avenue d'Eprémesnil, 78400 Chatou.
Colmar Ecole Mathias Grünewald, 4 rue Herzog, Logelbach-Wintzenheim, 68000 Colmar.
Laboissière Ecole Internat Rudolf Steiner, Laboissière-en-Thalle, 60570 Andeville.
Pau L'eau Vive 4 Avenue Edouard VII, 64000 Pau.
Saint Genis Laval Ecole Rudolf Steiner, 5 Chemin de Sanzy, 69230 St. Genis Laval.
Saint-Menoux Ecole Rudolf Steiner, Château de la Mothe, 03210 Saint-Menoux.
Strasbourg Ecole Libre Rudolf Steiner, 67e route des Romaines, 67200 Strasbourg-Koenigschofen.
Strasbourg Ecole Rudolf Steiner, 2 Chemin Goeb, 67000 Strasbourg.
Troyes Ecole Perceval, 214 Fg. Croncels, 10000 Troyes.
Verrières le Buisson Ecole Rudolf Steiner, 62 rue de Paris, Amblainvilliers, 91370 Verrières-le-Buisson.

GERMANY
Bund der Freien Waldorfschulen e.V., D-7000 Stuttgart 1, Heidehofstraße 32.
Aachen Freie Waldorfschulen Aachen, Aachener und Münchener Allee 5, D-5100 Aachen.
Augsburg Freie Waldorfschule Augsburg, Dr.-Schmelzing-Straße 52, D-8900 Augsburg.
Bad Nauheim Freie Waldorfschule Wetterau, Frankfurter Straße 103, 6350 Bad Nauheim.
Balingen Freie Waldorfschule Balingen, Hurdnagelstraße 3, D-7460 Baligen-Frommern.
Benefeld Freie Waldorfschule Landschulheim Benefeld, D-3036 Bomlitz-Benefeld üb. Walsrode/Hann.
Bergisch Gladbach Freie Waldorfschule Bergisch Gladbach, Mohnweg 62c Refrath, D-5060 Bergisch Gladbach 1.
Berlin-Dahlem Rudolf Steiner Schule Berlin e.V., Auf dem Grat 3, D-1000 Berlin 33.
Berlin-Zehlendorf Emile Molt Schule, Freie Waldorfschule, Claszeile 60-66, D-1000 Berlin 37 (Zehlendorf).
Berlin-Kreutzberg Emile Molt Schule, Freie Waldorfschule, Standort Kreutzberg, Alte Jakobstr. 12, D-1000 Berlin 61.
Berlin-Märkisch Viertel Waldorfschule Märkisches Viertel, Treuenbrietzenerstraße 28, D-1000 Berlin 26.
Berlin-Nord c/o Rudolf Steiner Schule Berlin e.V., Auf dem Grat, D-1000 Berlin 33.
Bexbach Freie Waldorfschule Saar-Pfalz, Parkstraße, D-6652 Bexbach.
Bielefeld Rudolf Steiner Schule Bielefeld, An der Probstei 23, D-4800 Bielefeld 1.
Bochum Rudolf Steiner Schule Bochum, Hauptstrasse 238, D-4630 Bochum 7.
Bonn Freie Waldorfschule Bonn, Stettiner Straße 21, D-5300 Bonn 1 (Tannenbusch).

Braunschweig Freie Waldorfschule Braunschweig, Rudolf-Steiner-Straße 2, D-3300 Braunschweig.

Bremen Freie Waldorfschule Bremen, Touler Straße 3, D-2800 Bremen 1.

Bremen Freie Waldorschule Bremen, Zweigschule Parsevalstraße 2, 2800 Bremen 44.

Chiemgau Freie Waldorfschule Chiemgau, Bernauer Straße 34, D-8210 Prien.

Coburg Rudolf Steiner Schule Coburg, Callenberg 12, D-8630 Coburg.

Darmstadt Freie Waldorfschule Darmstadt, Arndtstraße 6, D-6100 Darmstadt-Eberstadt.

Detmold Freie Waldorfschule Lippe-Detmold, Dresdener Straße 1, D-4930 Detmold.

Dortmund Rudolf Steiner Schule, Mergelteich-straße 51, D-4600 Dortmund 50.

Düsseldorf Rudolf Steiner Schule, Düsseldorf, Diepenstraße 15, D-4000 Düsseldorf 12.

Duisberg Freie Waldorschule Niederrhein, Am Nünninghof 11, 4100 Duisburg 18.

Eckerförde see Rendberg.

Elmshorn see Kiel.

Engelberg Freie Waldorfschule Engelberg, Rudolf-Steiner-Weg 4, D-7065 Engelberg, Post Winterbach/Württ.

Erlagen Freie Waldorfschule Erlangen, Zeißstraße 51, D-8520 Erlangen.

Essen Freie Waldorfschule, Schellstraße 47, D-4300 Essen 1.

Esslingen Freie Waldorfschule Esslingen, Weilstraße 90, D-7300 Esslingen.

Evinghausen Freie Waldorfschule Evinghausen, D-4550 Bramsche 8 (Evinghausen).

Filderstadt Freie Waldorfschule auf den Filden, Gutenhalde, D-7024 Filderstadt.

Flensburg Freie Waldorschule Flensburg, Valentiner Alle 1, D-2390 Flensburg.

Frankenthal Freie Waldorschule Vorderpfalz, Lilienstr. 10, D-6710 Frankenthal.

Frankfurt Freie Waldorfschule, Friedlebenstraße 52, D-6000 Frankfurt 50 (Eschersheim).

Freiburg Freie Waldorfschule Freiburg i. Br., Schwimmbadstraße 29, D-7800 Freiburg i. Br.

Freiburg Freie Waldorfschule St. Georgen, Bergiselstraße 11, D-7800 Freiburg.

Freiburg Michael-Schule, Kartäuserstraße 55, D-7800 Freiburg.

Gladbeck Freie Waldorfschule Gladbeck, Horsterstraße 82, D-4390 Gladbeck.

Göppingen Freie Waldorfschule Filstal, Ahornstraße 41, D-7320 Göppingen-Faurndau.

Göttingen Freie Waldorfschule Göttingen, Arbecksweg 1, D-3400 Göttingen.

Haan-Gruiten Freie Waldorfschule Haan-Gruiten, Prälat Marschallstraße 34, D-5657 Haan-2.

Hagen Rudolf Steiner Schule Hagen, Enneper Straße 30, D-5800 Hagen-Haspe.

Hamburg-Bergedorf Rudolf Steiner Schule Bergedorf, Am Brink 7, D-2050 Hamburg 80.

Hamburg-Bergstedt Rudolf Steiner Schule in den Walddörfern e.V. Hamburg-Bergstedt, Bergstedter Chaussee 207, D-2000 Hamburg 65.

Hamburg-Harburg Rudolf Steiner Schule Harburg, Ehestorfer Heuweg 82, D-2104 Hamburg 92.

Hamburg-Mitte Rudolf Steiner Schule Hamburg-Mitte e.V. Grabenstraße 32, D-2000 Hamburg 6.

Hamburg-Nienstedten Rudolf Steiner Schule Nienstedten, Elbchaussee 366, D-2000 Hamburg 52.

Hamburg-Wandsbek Rudolf Steiner Schule Wandsbek, Rahistedterweg 60, D-2000 Hamburg 72 (Farmsen).

Hamm Freie Waldorfschule Hamm, Feidikstraße 27, D-4700 Hamm 1.

Hannover Freie Waldorfschule, Rudolf-von-Bennigsen-Ufer 70, D-3000 Hannover 1.

Hannover-Bothfeld Freie Waldorfschule Hannover-Bothfeld, Weidkampshaide 17, D-3000 Hannover 51.

Heidleberg Freie Waldorfschule Heidleberg, Mittelgewannweg 16, D-6900 Heidleberg-Wieblingen.

Heidenheim Freie Waldorfschule , Ziegelstraße 50, Postfach 1340, D-7920 Heidenheim/Brenz.

Heilbronn Freie Waldorfschule Heilbronn, Max-von-Laue-Straße 4, D-7100 Heilbronn.

Hildesheim Freie Waldorfschule Hildesheim, Brauhausstraße 6, D-3200 Hildesheim.

Kakenstorf Rudolf Steiner Schule, Nordheide, Lange Straße 2, D-2117 Kakenstorf.

Karlsruhe Freie Waldorfschule Karlsruhe, Königsberger Straße 35a, D-7500 Karlsruhe 1.

Kassel Freie Waldorfschule Kassel (einschl. Berufsbildendes Gemeinschaftswerk mit Ausbildung für Facharbeiter und staatl. anerk. Erzieher), Hunrodstraße 17, D-3500 Kassel-Wilhelmshöhe.

Kiel Freie Waldorfschule Kiel, Hofholzallee 20, D-2300 Kiel 1.

Kiel/Elmshorn Freie Waldorfschule Kiel, Zweigschule Elmshorn, Bismarckstraße 13, D-2200 Elmshorn.

Kiel/Itzehoe Freie Waldorfschule Kiel, Zweigschule Itzehoe, Am Kählerhof, D-2210 Itzehoe/Holstein.

Kiel/Kaltenkirchen Freie Waldorfschule Kiel, Zweigschule Kaltenkirchen, Oersdorfer Weg 2, D-2358 Kaltenkirchen.

Köln Freie Waldorfschule Köln, Martinustraße 28, D-5000 Köln 71 (Esch.).

Krefeld Freie Waldorfschule Krefeld, Kaiser-straße 61, D-4150 Krefeld.

Loheland Rudolf Steiner Schule Loheland, D-6411 Künzell 5/Fulda.

Ludwigsburg Freie Waldorfschule Ludwigsburg, Fröbelstraße 16, D-7140 Ludwigsburg-Eglosheim.

Lübeck Freie Waldorfschule Lübeck, Dieselstraße 18, D-2400 Lübeck-Eichholz.

Lüneburg Rudolf Steiner Schule Lüneburg, Dahlenburger Landstraße 151, D-2120, Lüneburg.

Mainz Freie Waldorfschule Mainz, Merkurweg 2, D-6500 Mainz-Finthen.

Mannheim Freie Waldorfschule, Neckarauer Waldweg 131, D-6800 Mannheim 24.

Marburg Freie Waldorfschule Marburg, Ockerhäuser Allee 14, D-3550 Marburg/Lahn.

Mönchen-gladbach Rudolf Steinerschule in Mönchengladbach, Myllendonker Straße 113, D-4050 Mönchengladbach 1.

Mülheim/Ruhr Freie Waldorfschule in Mülheim, Blumendellerstraße 29, D-4330 Mülheim/Ruhr.

Mülheim Freie Waldorfschule im Markgräfler Land, D-7840 Mülheim.

München Rudolf Steiner Schule, Leopoldstraße 17, D-8000 München 40.

München-Gröbenzell Rudolf Steiner Schule München, Schulhaus Gröbenzell, Spechtweg 1, D-8038 Grobenzell.

München/Daglfing Rudolf Steiner Schule, Zweigschule Daglfing, Max-Proebstl-Straße 7, D-8000 München 81.

Münster Freie Waldorfschule Münster, Laerer Landweg 153-157, D-4440 Münster.

Neu-Isenburg Rudolf Steiner Schule Neu-Isenburg, Zeppelinstraße 10, D-6078 Neu-Isenburg.

Neuwied Rudolf Steiner Schule Mittelrhein 10, D-5450 Neuwied-Block.

Nürnberg Rudolf Steiner Schule, Steinplatten-weg 25, D-8500 Nürnberg.

Nürtingen Rudolf Steiner Schule, Erlenweg 1, D-7440 Nürtingen.

Offenburg Freie Waldorfschule Offenburg, Rheinstraße 3, D-7600 Offenburg.

Oldenburg Freie Waldorfschule, Blumenhof 9, D-2900 Oldenburg.

Ottersberg Freie Rudolf Steiner Schule, Amts-hof 5, D-2802 Ottersberg 1.

Pforzheim Goetheschule—Freie Waldorfschule, Schwarzwaldstraße 66, D-7530 Pforzheim.

Remscheid Rudolf Steiner Schule Remscheid, Schwarzer Weg 3, D-5630 Remscheid 11.
Rendsburg Freie Waldorfschule, Nobiskrüger Allee 75/77, D-2370 Rendsburg.
Rendsburg/Eckernförde Freie Waldorfschule Rendsburg, Zweigschule Eckernförde, Schleswiger Straße 112, D-2330 Eckernförde.
Reutlingen Freie Georgenschule, Moltkestraße 29, D-7410 Reutlingen.
Saarbrücken Freie Waldorfschule Saarbrücken, Großwaldstraße 2, D-6623 Altenkessel.
Schloß Hamborn Rudolf Steiner Schule Landschulheim Schloß Hamborn D-4799 Borchen-Schloß Hamborn.
Schondorf Rudolf Steiner Schule Ammersee, St.-Anna-Straße 15, D-8913 Schondorf/Ammersee.
Schopfheim Freie Waldorschule Schopfheim, Schlierbachstraße 23, D-7860 Schopfheim.
Schwäbisch Gmünd Freie Waldorfschule Schwäbisch Gmünd, Scheffoldstraße 136-140, D-7070 Schwäbische Gmünd.
Schwäbisch Hall Freie Waldorschule Schwäbisch Hall, Teuererweg 2, D-7170 Schwäbische Hall.
Siegen Rudolf Steiner Schule Siegen, Kolpingstraße 3, D-5900 Siegen.
Stuttgart Freie Waldorfschule Uhlandshöhe, Haußmannstraße 44, D-7000 Stuttgart 1.
Stuttgart Freie Waldorfschule am Kräherwald, Rudolf-Steiner-Weg 10, D-7000 Stuttgart 1.
Stuttgart Michael Bauer Schule, Freie Waldorfschule mit Förderklassenbereich, Othellostraße 5, D-7000 Stuttgart 80.
Trier Freie Waldorfschule, Montessoriweg 7, D-5500 Trier.
Tübingen Tübingen Freie Waldorfschule, Rotdornweg 30, D-7400 Tübingen-Waldhäuser-Ost.
Überlingen Freie Waldorfschule am Bodensee, D-7770 Überlingen-Rengoldshausen.
Ulm Freie Waldorfschule Ulm mit angeschlossene Sonderklassen für Lernbehinderte, Römerstraße 97, D-7900 Ulm.
Ulm Freie Waldorfschule am Illerblick, Untere Kuhberg 22, D-7900 Ulm.
Vaihingen/Enz Freie Waldorschule Vaihingen/Enz, Franckstraße 30, D-7143 Vaihingen/Enz.
Villengen-Schwenningen Rudolf Steiner Schule, Schluchseestraße 55, D-7730 VS-Schwenningen.
Wahlwies Freie Waldorfschule Wahlwies, D-7768 Stockach 14.
Wangen Freie Waldorfschule Wangen, Rudolf-Steiner-Straße 4, D-7988 Wangen i. Allgäu.
Wanne-Eickel Hiberniaschule, Holsterhäuser Straße 70, Postfach 2849, D-4690 Herne 2.
Wattenscheid Widar Schule Wattenscheid, Höntroper Straße 95, D-4630 Bochum 6.
Wernstein Freie Waldorfschule Wernstein, Patersbergweg 5-7, D-8651 Wernstein.
Wiesbaden Freie Waldorfschule Wiesbaden, Kohlheckstraße 43, D-6200 Wiesbaden.
Witten Rudolf Steiner Schule Witten, Billerbeckstraße 2, D-5810 Witten-Heven.
Witten Rudolf Steiner Schule Witten, Bochumer Straße 10a, D-5810 Witten-Heven.
Wolfsburg Freie Waldorfschule Wolfsburg e.V., Masurenweg 9, D-3180 Wolfsburg 1.
Würzburg Freie Waldorfschule Würzburg, Oberer Neubergweg 14, D-8700 Würzburg.
Wuppertal Christian Morgenstern Schule, Waldorfschule für Erziehungshilfe, Haderslebener Straße 14, D-5600 Wuppertal 2 (Barmen).
Wuppertal West Freie Waldorfschule Wuppertal-West, Schluchtstraße 21, D-5600 Wuppertal 2.

ITALY

Albano Libera Scuola de Castelle Romani, Via Cipressetti 6, Ariccia 00041
Meran Freie Waldorfschule Villa Steinling, Schennastraße 47 A, 39012 Meran.

Milano Scuola Rudolf Steiner, Via Celeste Clericetti 45, 20/33 Milano.
Oriago Scuola Steineriano, Riveria Bocso Piccolo 40, 30030 Oriago di Mira (Venezia).
Roma Scuola Rudolf Steiner 'Giardino del Cedri', Via delle Benedettine 10, 00135 Roma.
Trieste Scuola Rudolf Steiner, Via Trento 12, 34132 Trieste.

LUXEMBOURG
Luxembourg Fräi-Öffentlech-Waldorschoul Lëtzebeurg, 6, Avenue Joseph Sax, Luxembourg-Limpeertsberg.

NETHERLANDS
Band der Vrije Scholen in Nederland Secretariaat: Hoofdstraat 20, 3972 Driebergen.
* Incl. Upper School   Only Kindergarten.
Alkmaar Rudolf Steinerschool, Sperwerstraat 1, 1826 KL.
Alkmaar Rudolf Steinerschool — Oudorp, Raadhuisstraat 3, 1829 BT.
* **Alkmaar** Frije School Bovenbouw, Loudels-weg 24, Postbus 222, 1860 AE Bergen.
Almelo Vrije School Almelo, Biesterweg 6, 7608 RN.
Almere Vrije School, Heerlenstraat 33A, 1324 MC.
Alphen A/D Rijn Vrije School, Hoefbladstrat 46, Postbus 1032, 2400 AD.
Amersfoort Vrije School, Romeostraat 74, 3816 SE.
Amstelveen Parcivalschool, Lindenlaan 317, 1185 LM.
* **Amsterdam** Geert Grooteschool, Hygiëaplein 47, 1076 RS.
Apeldoorn Vrije School, Morinistraat 6, 7312 KC.
Arnhem Percivalschool, Woudrichemstraat 141, Postbus 30093, 6803 AB.
Assen Vrije School Koekkoekstr. 17, 9404 BL.
* **Bergen** Vrije School, Prins Hendriklaan 58, 1882 EL.
Bergen Vrije School Bovenbouw, van de Veldelaan 179, 1860 AE Bergen.
Bilthoven Rudolf Steinerschool, Weltevreden 6, Postbus 332, 3720 AH.
Den Bosch Rudolf Steinerschool, Waalstraat 30, 5215 CK.
Boxmeer Vrije School, Van Cootstraat 34, 5831 Hl.
Breda Rudolf Steinerschool, Minckelerstraat 27, 4816 AD.
Bussum Vrije School Michaël, Ester de Boer van Rijklaan 22, 1403 GD.
Delft Vrije School, De Meesterstraat 2, 2613 XB.
Deventer Vrije School, Oosterstraat 3a, 7411 XV.
Dordrecht Vrije School, Dubbelmondestraat 1, 3311 NB.
* **Driebergen** Vrije School, Faunalaan 250, Postbus 207, 3970 AE.
Ede Vrije School, Nachtegaallaan 47a-49, Postbus 40, 6710 BA.
* **Eindhoven** Vrije School Brabant, Woenselsestraat 316, Postbus 1073, 5602 BB.
Eindhoven-Zuid Vrije School, Hadewychlaan 3, 5643 RT.
Emmen De Vrije School Michael, Prinsenlaan 80, 7822 CF Emmen.
Gouda Vrije School, Ridder v. Catsweg 256a, 2805 BC.
* **Groningen** De Vrije School Bovenbouw, Merwedestraat 98, 9718 KG.
* **Den Haag** Vrije School, Waalsdorperweg 12, 2597 JB.
Den Helder Vrije School, Reggestraat 38, 1784 XN.
* **Haarlem** Rudolf Steinerschool, Engelandlaan 2, 2034 NA.
Haarlem-Noord Vrije School Kennemerland, Weltevredenstraat 9, Postbus 2161, 2002 CD.
Harderwijk de Valentijnschool, B. Toussainstr. 1, 3842 ZZ Ermelo.
Helmond Vrije School Peelland, Helmonselaan 71, 5702 NM.
Hilversum Vrije School, Oude Amerfoortseweg 198, Postbus 1643, 1200 BP.
Hoorn Westfriese Vrije School, Nachtegaall 146, 1628 DJ.

Krimpen A/S Ijssel Krimpener Vrije School, Hobbemalaan 2, 2923 XH.
Leeuwarden Michaëlschool, Nieuwe Schrans 11a, Postbus 1140, 8900 CC.
Leiden Rudolf Steinerschool, César Franck-straat 9, 2324 JM.
Leiden-Noord Vrije School Mareland, Maresingel 19, 2316 HA.
* **Leiden** Vrije Schoolgemeensch. Rudolf Steiner, Surinamestraat 1, 2315 XC.
Maastricht Vrije School, Heugemer Pastoorstraat 12, Postbus 1017, 6201 BA.
Meppel Vrije School, Julianastraat 22, 7941 JC.
* **Middelburg** Vrije School Zeeland, Willem Arondeusstraat 59, 4333 DD.
Middelburg Bovenbouw Vrije School Zeeland, Gravenstraat 63, 4331 NL.
* **Nijmegen** Steinerschool, Meyhorst 24-74/76, 6537 GR.
Nijmegen Vrije School 'Oost', Groesbeekseweg 146, 6525 DN.
* **Nijmegen** Regionale Bovenbouw, Wilheminasingel 15, 6542 AJ.
* **Oldenzaal** Vrije School, Jacob Catsstraat 2, 7576 BS.
Oosterhout Vrije School, Brabantlaan 7, Postbus 4010, 4900 CA.
Oud Beijerland Vrije School Hoeksche Waard, Jasmijnstraat 6, Postbus 1176, 3620 AD.
Roermond Vrije School, Christophorus, Schouwberg 27, 6041 AG Leeuwen/Roermond.
Rosendaal Vrije School Rosendaal, Gerard ten Borchstraat 39, 4037 NL.
* **Rotterdam** Vrije School, Vredehofweg 30, Postbus 4292, 3006 AG.
Rotterdam Vrije School Prinsenland, Michaelangelostraat 375, Postbus 4292, 3006 AG.
Rotterdam Vrije School Bovenbouw, Vondelweg 87-89, Postbus 4292, 3006 AG.
Den Burg Texel Vrije School Texel, Gasthuisstraat 55, Postbus 6, 1790 AA.
Tiel Johannesschool, Postbus 393, 4000 AJ.
Tilburg Vrije School, Wilhelminapark 54, 5041 ED.
Uden Vrije School, Bosveld 122, Postbus 139, 5400AC.
Utrecht Vrije School, Hieronymusplantsoen 3, 3512 KV.
Venlo Rudolf Steinerschool, Noord-Limburg, Zusterstraat 5, 5914 XX VENLO.
Voorschoten Rudolf Steiner Kleuterschool, Burg. de Koolplantsoen 19, 2253 KD.
Wageningen Vrije School de Zwaneridder, Nolenstraat 3, Postbus 508, 6700 AM.
Winterswijk Vrije School, Wielwaalstraat 2, 7102 HB.
Zaandam Vrije School Zaanstreek, Galjoen-straat 111B, 1503 AR.
Zeist Zeister Vrije School, Socrateslaan 22, 3707 GL.
* **Zeist** Strichtse Vrije School, Regional Bovenbouw, Socrateslaan 22, 3707 GL.
Zoetermeer Vrije School, Schansbos 5-6, 2716 GV.
Zutphen Vrije School 'de Ijssel', Henri Dunantweg 4, 7201 EV.
Zutphen Vrije School 'de Berkel', Weerdslag 14b, 7206 BR.
* **Zutphen** Vrije School Bovenbouw 'de Ijssel', Isendoornstraat 22, 7201 NJ.
Zwolle Vrije School, Bachlaan 6-8, 8031 HL.

NEW ZEALAND

Auckland Michael Park School K-12, 55 Amy Street Ellerslie, P.O. Box 28-150, Remuera, Auckland 5.
Auckland Titirangi Rudolf Steiner School K-6, Armour Bay Road, Parau, P.O. Box 60-266, Titirangi, Auckland 7.
Christchurch Christchurch Rudolf Steiner School K-12, 19 Ombersley Terrace, Opawa, Christchurch 2.
Dunedin Kotuku School K-2, 95 Norwood Street, Normanby, Dunedin.
Hastings Rudolf Steiner School K-12, 415N Nelson Street, P.O. Box 888, Hastings.
Wellington Raphael House Rudolf Steiner School K-7, 27 Matuhi Street, Belmont, Lower Hutt, Wellington.

NORWAY
Steinerskole i Norge. Secretary: Postboks 25, 0705 Oslo 7.
Ålesund Steinerskolen i Ålesund, Moa, 6018 Ålesund.
Asker Rudolf Steinerskolen i Asker, Nesvangen 10, 1360 Nesbru.
Askim Steinerskolen i Indre Östfold, Holterveien 75, 1800 Askim.
Baerum Steinerskolen i Baerum, Grav Gårdsvej 5, N 1342 Jar.
Bergen Rudolf Steiner-Skolen i Bergen, Rieber-Mohns vej 15, 5040 Paradis.
Bergen Steinerskolen på Nesttun, Postboks 317, 5051 Nesttun.
Drammen Steinerskolen i Drammen, Glydenlıves plass 1, 3000 Drammen.
Fredrickstad Steinerskolen i Frederickstad, Nabbetorpveien 99, Boks 1188, 1601
Fredrickstad.
Gjövik/Toten Steinerskolen Gjövik/Toten, Kap Melkfabrikker, 2858 Kapp.
Haugesund Steinerskolen i Haugesund, Solvang, 5500 Haugesund.
Hedmarken Steinerskolen i Hedmarken, Kjonerudgård, Boks 100, 2310 Ottestad.
Hurum Rudolf Steinerskolen i Hurum, Holtebrekk, 3490 Klokkarstua.
Lillehammaer Lillehammer Steinerskolen, Fåberggt 152, 2600 Lillehammer.
Lırenskog Steinerskolen i Lırenskog, Postboks 13, 1473 Skårer.
Moss Rudolf Steinerskolen i Moss, Boks 3045, 1501 Moss.
Nesoddtangen Rudolf Steinerskolen på Nesodden, Eysteins vei 4B, 1450 Nesoddtangen.
Nestun Steinerskolen på Nestun, Postboks 317, 5051 Nestun.
Oslo Rudolf Steinerskolen i Oslo, Postboks 25, Hovseter, 0705, Oslo 7.
Ringerike Rudolf Steinerskolen på Ringerike, Alm gård, 3520 Jevnaker.
Rygge Steinerskolen i Rygge, Boks 130, 1510 Rygge.
Stavanger Steinerskolen i Stavanger, Nylundsgt 1, 4000 Stavanger.
Trondheim Steinerskolen i Trondheim, Postboks 3521, 7001 Trondheim.
Tromsö Steinerskolen i Tromsö, Inga Sparboes vei 41, 9000 Tromsö.
Vestfold Steinerskolen i Vestfold, Postboks 10, Vestkogen, 3140 Borgheim.

PERU
Lima Collegio Waldorf Lima, Aptdo. 03-0164, Salamenca, Lima 3.

SOUTH AFRICA
Southern African Federation of Waldorf Schools—
Secretariat: Waldorf School, Constantia.
Alexandra Inkanyezi Waldorfschool, P.O. Box 2302, Rivonia 2128, Transvaal.
Cape Town Waldorf School, Spaanschemat River Road, Constantia 7800.
Cape Town Michael Oak Waldorf School, 4 Marlow Road, 7700 Kenilworth, Cape
Town.
Durban Natal Waldorf School, P.O. Box 503, Hilcrest 3650.
Johannesburg Michael Mount Waldorf School, P.O. Box 67587, Bryanston, 2021.
Pretoria Max Stibbe School, 257 Mooiplaas, P.O. Box 11384, Brooklyn 0011,
Pretoria/Transvaal.

SPAIN
Madrid Escuela Libre Micael, Carretera de la Coruna, km. 22, Apartado de Correoa
13, SP-28230 Las Rozas, Madrid.

SWEDEN
Delsbo Delsbo Waldorfskolan, Box 71, S-82060 Delsbo.

Delsbo Sofiaskolan, Rudolf Steinerskolan, Fuyrugatan 1 S-82060 Delsbo.
Garpenberg Annaskolan, Dormsjö 808, S-77073 Garpenberg.
Göteborg Rudolf Steinerskolan, Birkagatan 61, S-41656 Göteborg.
Järna Nibbleskolan, Solvik, S-15300 Järna.
Järna Örjanskolan, Rudolf Steinerskola i Järna, Nibble, S-15300 Järna.
Järna Maria-Magdalena-skolen, Parkvägen 11, S-15300 Järna.
Kalmar Kalmar Waldorfskola, Drottning Blankes Väg 10 393, 52 Kalmar.
Kungälv Fredkullaskolan, Fontinvägen 37, S-44231 Kungälv.
Linköping Steinerskolan, Munkhagsgaten 60c, S-58256 Linköping.
Lund Rudolf Steinerskolan i Lund, Box 31, S-24107 Södra Sandby.
Märsta Josefinaskolan, Stockholmsvägen 42, S-19532 Märsta.
Norrköping Rudolf Steinerskolan i Norrköping, Box 748, S-60116 Norrköping.
Nyköping Mikaeliskolan, Hospitalgatan 31, S-61132 Nyköping.
Örebro Johannaskolan—Örebro Waldorfskola, Glomman 94, S-70230 Örebro.
Simrishamm Sofiaskolan, Rörum, S-27294 Simrishamm.
Söderköping Waldorfskola i Söderköping, Hammarspången, S-61400 Söderköping.
Spånga Ellen Key Skolan, Stockholms Norrra Waldorfskola, Duvbovägen 94, S-16358, Spånga.
Stockholm Kristofferskolan, Box 124, S-16126 Bromma.
Stockholm Martinskolan, Söders Waldorfskola, Munstycksvägen 18, S-12357 Farsta.
Umeå Umeå Waldorfskola, PL 5285, S-90251 Umeå.
Västerås Mariaskolan Viksängsgatan 76, S-72347 Västerås.

SWITZERLAND
Adliswil/Zürich Rudolf-Steiner-Schule Sihlau, Sihlstr. 23, CH 8134 Adliswil/ZH.
Aesch Rudolf-Steiner-Schule Birseck, Apfelseestraße 1, CH 4147 Aesch.
Basel Rudolf-Steiner-Schule, Jakobsberger Holzweg 54, CH 4509 Basel.
Basel Christophorus Schule, Förderschule, Bürrenfluhstraße. 20, CH. 4059 Basel.
Basel Helfenbergschule, Förderschule, Starenstraße 41, CH 4059 Basel.
Basel Neue Rudolf Steiner Schule Basel, D. Ackermann, Maulbeerstraße 18, CH 4058 Basel.
Bern Rudolf-Steiner-Schule Bern, Ittigenstraße 31, CH 3063 Ittigen.
Biel Rudolf-Stener-Schule, Rosenheimweg 1, CH 2502 Biel.
Chur Rudolf-Steiner-Schule Chur, Münzweg 20, CH 7000 Chur.
St. Gallen Rudolf-Steiner-Schule, Zwilingstraße 25, CH 9000 St. Gallen.
Geneva/Confignon Ecole Rudolf Steiner, Ch. de Narly 2, CH 1232 Confignon.
Glarisegg Freie Bildungstätte Glarisegg, Waldorfinternat für Oberstrufe, CH 8266 Steckborn.
Ins 'Schlössli' Ins, Rudolf-Steiner-Schule, CH 3232 Ins/BE.
Kreuzlingen Rudolf-Steiner-Schule, Bahnhofstraße 15, CH 8280 Kreuzlingen.
Langenthal Rudolf-Steiner-Schule Oberaargau, Ringstraße 30, CH 4900 Langenthal.
Langnau Rudolf-Steiner-Schule Oberemmental, Schloss-Straße 6, CH 3550 Langnau.
Lausanne Ecole Rudolf Steiner de Lausanne, La Longeraie, CH 1110 Morges/VD.
Lenzburg Rudolf-Steiner-Schule Aargau, Alte Bernstrasse, CH 5503 Schafisheim.
Lugano Scuola Rudolf Steiner, Centro Nord/Sud. Via Campagna, CH 6934 Bioggio.
Luzern Rudolf-Steiner-Schule, Kantonsspital 21, CH 6000 Luzern.
Neuchatel Ecole Rudolf Steiner, La Coudraie, CH 2206 Les Geneveys-sur-Coffrane.
Pratteln Rudolf-Steiner-Schule Mayenfels, Schloß Mayenfels, CH 4133 Pratteln.
Schaffhausen Rudolf-Steiner-Schule, Vordersteig 24, CH 8200 Schaffhausen.

Schuls-Tarasp Rudolf-Steiner-Schule, CH 7553 Tarasp bei Scuol, Unterengadin.
Solothurn Rudolf-Steiner-Schule, Allmendstraße 75, CH 4500 Solothurn.
Spiez Rudolf-Steiner-Schule Berner Oberland, Mühlegässli 18, CH 3700 Spiez.
Wetzikon Rudolf-Steiner-Schule, Zürcher Oberland, Usterstrasse 141, CH 8621 Wetzikon.
Wil Freie Volksschule Wil, Säntisstr. 31, CH 9500 Wil.
Winterthur Rudolf-Steiner-Schule, Maienstraße 15, CH 8406 Winterthur.
Zürich Rudolf-Steiner-Schule, Plattenstraße 37, CH 8032 Zürich.
Zürich-Albisrieden Rudolf-Steiner-Schule, Albisrieden, Bockhornstraße 3, CH 8047 Zürich.
Zug Rudolf-Steiner-Schule Zug, Asylstraße 15, CH 6340 Baar.

UNITED KINGDOM AND IRELAND

Steiner Schools Fellowship, Kidbrooke Park, Forest Row, East Sussex RH18 5JB. Tel. (0342) 822115.

* Full Membership of Steiner Schools Fellowship.
† Associated Schools.
χ Newly Founded Schools.
k Playgroup and/or Kindergarten recognised by Steiner Kindergarten Steering Group.

Aberdeen † Aberdeen Waldorf School, 111 Gallowgate, Aberdeen AB1 1BU. Tel. (0224) 646111.
Belfast* Holywood School, 34 Croft Road, Holywood, County Down BT18 0PR. Tel. (0232) 428029.
Botton* Botton Village School, Danby, Whitby, North Yorks YO21 2NJ. Tel. (0287) 661204.
Brighton † Brighton Steiner School, 363 Ditchling Road, Brighton, Sussex BN1 6JU. Tel. (0273) 260440.
Bristol* Bristol Waldorf School, Park Place, Clifton, Bristol BS8 1JR. Tel (0272) 260440.
Canterbury* Perry Court School, Garlinge Green, Chartham, Canterbury, Kent CT4 5RU. Tel. (0227) 738285.
Cooleenbridge χ Cooleenbridge School, Feakle, Co. Clare, Eire. Tel. (010 353) 61921494.
Dublin χ Dublin Rudolf Steiner School, 28 Maxwell Road, Rathmines, Dublin 6. Tel: (0001) 517834.
Dyfed † Nant-y-Cwm Steiner School, Llanycefn, Clynderwen, Dyfed SA66 7QJ. Tel. (0437) 563640.
Edinburgh* The Rudolf Steiner School of Edinburgh, 38 Colinton Road, Edinburgh EH10 5BT. Tel. (031) 337 3410.
Forest Row* Michael Hall School, Kidbrooke Park, Forest Row, East Sussex RH18 5JB. Tel. (0342) 822275.
Glasgow χ Glasgow Steiner School, Govan Business Centre, 49 Harhill Street, Govan, Glasgow G51 3NL. Tel. (041) 445 2372.
Gloucester* Wynstones School, Whaddon Green, Gloucester GL4 0UF. Tel. (0452) 522475.
Hereford † Hereford Waldorf School, Much Dewchurch, Hereford HR2 8DE. Tel. (0981) 540221.
Ilkeston* Michael House School, The Field, Shipley, Heanor, Derbyshire DE7 7JH. Tel. (0773) 718050.

Kings Langley* Rudolf Steiner School, Langley Hill, Kings Langley, Herts WD4 9HG. Tel. (0923) 262505.

London *k* Mulberry Bush Kindergarten, c/o 19 Jeffreys Place, London NW1 9PP. Tel. (071) 485 9859.

London χ North London Rudolf Steiner School, P.O. Box 280, London N8 7HT. Tel. (081) 348 5050.

London *k* Primrose Nursery, 34 Glenila Road, London NW3 4AP. Tel. (071) 722 3587.

London χ Waldorf School of South West London, 12 Balham Park Road, London SW12 8DR. Tel. (081) 677 1763.

Morayshire Moray Steiner School, Drumduan, Clovenside Road, Forres, Morayshire IV36 0RD. Tel. (0309) 76300.

Oxford *k* Oxford Waldorf Kindergarten, The Old Primary School, Stanton St-John, Oxford OX9 1ET. Tel. (08677) 4558.

Reading *k* Reading Steiner School Kindergarten, Christchurch Gardens, Reading, Berks. Tel. (0734) 872396/585712.

Ringwood* Ringwood Waldorf School, Ashley, Ringwood, Hants BH24 2NN. Tel. (0425) 472664.

St. Albans *k* St. Albans Kindergarten, Fleetville Community Centre, 67 Hempstead Road, Kings Langley, Herts WD4 8BS. Tel. (0923) 762453.

Sheffield χ Sheffield Steiner School, 2 Meadow Bank Road, Sheffield SH11 9AH. Tel. (0742) 551638.

Snowdonia χ Snowdonia Steiner School, Plas Tan Yr Allt, Porthmadog, Tremadog, Gwynedd LL49 9RG. Tel. (0766) 512068.

Stourbridge* Elmfield School, Love Lane, Stourbridge, West Midlands DY8 2EA. Tel. (0384) 394663.

Stroud *k* Stroud Valleys Kindergarten, The Lindens, Stroud, Glos. GL5 2HT. Tel. (0452) 812393.

Stroud *k* Sunlands Nursery, Cainscross Road, Stroud, Glos. GL5 4EX. Tel. (0452) 813795.

Totnes † Rudolf Steiner School South Devon, Hood Manor, Dartington, Totnes, Devon TQ9 6AB. Tel. (080 426) 528.

Tunbridge Wells *k* Golden Spring Kindergarten, Subud Hall, 14 Culverden Down, Tunbridge Wells, Kent. Tel. c/o (0342) 823491.

York † York Steiner School, Fulford Cross, York Y01 4PB. Tel. (0904) 654983.

UNITED STATES OF AMERICA
* *Full member of the Association of Waldorf Schools of North America.*

CALIFORNIA

* **Auburn** Live Oak Waldorf School, K-6, P.O. Box 57, Applegate, CA 95703.

Altadena Pasadena Waldorf School, K-8, 209 East Mariposa Street, Altadena, CA 910001-5133.

* **Calpella** Mountain Meadow Country School, K-8, Box 349, 6280 3rd Street, Calpella, CA 94903.

Cedar Ridge Mariposa Waldorf School, K-5, P.O. Box 1210, Cedar Ridge, CA 95924.

* **Emeryville** East Bay Waldorf School, K-8, 1275 61st Street, Emeryville, CA 94608.

* **Fair Oaks** Sacramento Waldorf School, K-12, 3750 Bannister Road, Fair Oaks, CA 95628.

Fair Oaks Rudolf Steiner College (adult education), 9200 Fair Oaks Boulevard, Fair Oaks, CA 95628.

Los Altos Waldorf School of the Peninsula, K-7, 401 Rosita Avenue, Los Altos, CA 94022.
Monterey Waldorf School of Monterey, K-3, P.O. Box 221057, Carmel, CA 93922.
* **Northridge** Highland Hall, K-12, 17100 Superior Street, Northridge, CA 91325.
Northridge Waldorf Institute of Southern California (adult education), 171000 Superior Street, Northridge, CA 91325.
San Diego Waldorf School of San Diego, K-3, P.O. Box 7365, San Diego, CA 92107.
* **San Francisco** San Francisco Waldorf School, K-8, 2938 Washington Street, San Francisco, CA 94115.
* **San Rafael** Marin Waldorf School, K-8, 755 Idylberry Road, San Rafael, CA 94903.
Santa Barbara Waldorf School of Santa Barbara, K-5, 2300B Garden Street, Santa Barbara CA 93105.
* **Santa Cruz** Santa Cruz Waldorf School, K-8, 2190 Empire Grade, Santa Cruz, CA 95060.
* **Santa Rosa** Summerfield Waldorf School, K-12, 155 Willowside Road, Santa Rosa, CA 95401.
COLORADO
Boulder Shining Mountain Waldorf School, K-8, 987 Locust, Boulder, CO 80302.
* **Denver** Denver Waldorf School, K-8, 735 East Florida Avenue, Denver, CO 80210.
FLORIDA
Gainesville Gainesville Waldorf School, N-4, 921 SW Depot Avenue, Gainesville, FL 32601.
GEORGIA
Atlanta The Children's Garden, K, 2089 Ponce de Leon Avenue, Atlanta, GA 30307.
HAWAII
* **Honolulu**Honolulu Waldorf School, N-8, 350 Ulua Street, Honolulu, HI 96821.
Kealakekuo Pali Uli Waldorf School, K-3, Box 1338, Kealakekuo, HI 96750.
Keau Malamalama School, N-8, SR 13031, Keau, HI 96750.
Kilauea Kauai Waldorf School, K-3, P.O. Box 818, Kilauea, HI 96754.
* **Kula** Haleakela School, N-8, Route 1, Box 790, Kula, HI 96790.
ILLINOIS
* **Chicago** Chicago Waldorf School, N-8, 1651 West Diversey, Chicago, IL 60614.
MAINE
Freeport Merriconeag School, NK, P.O. Box 356, Freeport, ME 04032.
MARYLAND
* **Baltimore** Waldorf School of Baltimore, N-8, 4701 Yellowood Avenue, Baltimore, MD 21209.
* **Bethesda**Washington Waldorf School, N-12, 4800 Sangamore Road, Bethesda, MD 20816.
MASSACHUSETTS
Beverly Cape Ann School, N-4/5, 35 Conant Street, Beverely, MA 01915.
Falmouth Waldorf School of Cape Cod, N-4, P. O. Box 687/270 Old Main Road, No. Falmouth, MA 02543.
* **Great Barrington** Great Barrington Rudolf Steiner School K-8, West Plain Road, Great Barrington, MA 01230.
* **Hadley** Hartsbrook Waldorf School, N-6, 94 Bay Road, Hadley, MA 01035.
* **Lexington** Waldorf School, N-8, 739 Massachusetts Avenue, Lexington, MA 02173.
MICHIGAN
* **Ann Arbor** Rudolf Steiner School of Ann Arbor, K-8, 2775 Newport Road, Ann Arbor, MI 48103.

Bloomfield Hills Oakland Steiner School, N-3, 1000 Cranbrook Road, Bloomfield Hills, MI 48013.

* **Detroit** Detroit Waldorf School, K-8, 2555 Burns Avenue, Detroit, MI 48214.
MINNESOTA
Minneapolis Waldorf City School, N-3, 3114 W.49th Street, Minneapolis, MN 55426.
* **West St. Paul** Minnesota Waldorf School, K-6, 1037 Bidwell Street, West St. Paul, MN 55118.
NEW HAMPSHIRE
* **Keene** Monadnock Waldorf School, K-8, 98 South Lincoln St., Keene, NH 03431.
Keene Antioch/New England, Roxbury Street, Keene, NH 03431 (adult education).
* **Wilton** High Mowing School, 9-12, Wilton, NH 03086.
* **Wilton** Pine Hill Waldorf School, K-8, Wilton, NH 03086.
NEW JERSEY
Princeton Waldorf School of Princeton, K-7, 1062 Cherry Hill Road, RD # 3, Princeton, NJ 08540.
NEW MEXICO
Santa Fe Santa Fe Waldorf School, K-8, Rt. 9, Box 50-B3, Santa Fe, NM 87505.
NEW YORK.
* **Garden City** Waldorf School of Garden City, N-12, Cambridge Avenue, Garden City, NY 11530.
* **Ghent** Hawthorne Valley School, K-12, RD 2, Box 225, Ghent, NY 12075.
Ithaca Waldorf School of Finger Lakes, K-8, 855 Five Mile Drive, Ithaca, NY 14850.
New Paltz Mountain Laurel School, N-6, 304 Route 32 North, New Paltz, NY 12561.
* **New York** Rudolf Steiner School, K-12, 15 East 79th Street, New York, 10021.
Saratoga Springs Spring Hill School, N-6, 62-66 York Avenue, Saratoga Springs, NY 12866.
* **Spring Valley** Green Meadow School, K-12, Hungry Hollow Road, Spring Valley, NY 10977.
Spring Valley Waldorf Institute, 260 Hungry Hollow Road, Spring Valley, NY 10977 (adult education).
NORTH CAROLINA
Chapel Hill Emerson Waldorf School, K-7, 6211 New Jericho road, Chapel Hill, NC 27514.
OHIO
Akron Spring Garden School, N-8, 2141 Pickle Road, Akron, OH 44312.
Cincinnati Cincinnati Waldorf School, N-4, 2350 Ravine Street, Cincinnati, OH 45219.
OREGON
* **Eugene** Eugene Waldorf School, K-8, 1350 McClean Boulevard, Eugene, OR 97405.
Portland Portland Waldorf School, K-8, 7754 SW Capitol Highway, Portland, OR 97219-2477.
PENNSYLVANIA
* **Kimberton** Kimberton Waldorf School, K-12, West Seven Stars Road, Kimberton, PA 19442.
Marrietta Susquehanna Waldorf School, K-3, 15 Walnut Street/P.O. Box 165, Marietta, PA 17547.
RHODE ISLAND
West Kingston, Meadowbrook Waldorf School, K-2, P.O. Box 508, West Kingston, RI 02892.
TEXAS
* **Austin** Austin Waldorf School, K-8, 8702 South View Road, Austin, TX 78737.

VERMONT
Shelburne Lake Champlain Waldorf School, K-3, 27 Harbour Road, Shelburne, VT 05482.
Wolcott Green Mountain School, K-6, RP#1, Box 4885, Wolcott, VT 05680.
VIRGINIA
Charlottesville Crossroads Waldorf School, N-6, P.O. Box 5221, Charlottesville, VA 22905.
Richmond Richmond Waldorf School, K-5, 1704 W. Laburnum Ave. Richmond, VA 23227.
WASHINGTON
Bellingham Whatcom Hills Waldorf School, K-5, 941 Austin Street, Bellingham, WA 98226.
Clinton Chinook Waldorf School, K-3, P.O. Box 469, Clinton, WA 98236.
Olympia Olympia Waldorf School, K-6, P.O. Box 638, Olympia, WA 98540.
Seattle Seattle Waldorf School, N-8, 2728 N.E. 100th Street, Seattle, WA 98125.
WISCONSIN
Milwaukee Waldorf School of Milwaukee, N-4, 1603 North Cass Street, Milwaukee WI 53202.
New Berlin Prairie Hill Waldorf School, N-1 5150 South Sunny Slope Road, New Berlin, WI 53151.
Viroqua Pleasant Ridge School, N-6, 321 East Decker Street, Viroqua, WI 54665.

URUGUAY
Montevideo Colegio Novalis, Metodo Waldorf, Avenida Bolivia 2122, Montevideo.

This list is subject to constant revision and updating and may not be totally comprehensive and accurate in all its details.

RECOMMENDED FOR FURTHER READING

BY RUDOLF STEINER:

THE EDUCATION OF THE CHILD IN THE LIGHT OF ANTHROPOSOPHY

This early essay gives in seed form what later became the far-reaching Waldorf School Movement and provides an excellent introduction to Steiner's ideas on education.

ISBN: 0 85440 620 4   Booklet   £3.50

THE STUDY OF MAN

These lectures were given as a preparation for their task to the teachers of the original Waldorf school in Stuttgart, the first school to be founded on the work of Rudolf Steiner in 1919. They contain Steiner's fundamental views on the psychology of the developing human being.

ISBN: 0 85440 104 0   Cloth   £8.95
        0 85440 292 6   Paper   £5.95

PRACTICAL ADVICE TO TEACHERS

Like *The Study of Man*, these lectures form part of the basic training material given by Steiner to teachers of the first Waldorf school. With penetrating insight into the nature of the child, Steiner gives imaginative and practical suggestions for a wide variety of educational problems and situations.

ISBN: 0 85440 302 7   Cloth   £10.00
        0 85440 303 5   Paper   £6.95

A MODERN ART OF EDUCATION

These lectures form one of the most comprehensive introductions to the philosophy of Waldorf education. Steiner presents the need for a new ideal of the human being, his psychology of the child's growth and the rhythms apparent in the course of development. Suggestions are given as to how to present a variety of subjects to the child's developing consciousness.

ISBN: 0 85440 261 6   Cloth   £10.00
         0 85440 262 4   Paper   £6.95

THE KINGDOM OF CHILDHOOD

This is the last course Steiner gave for teachers — in this case for the prospective teachers of the school about to be established in London. More than in the earlier courses, the emphasis is on the practical application of teaching skills.

ISBN: 0 85440 284 5   Paper   £5.95

BY OTHER AUTHORS

THE WAY OF A CHILD
A. C. Harwood

This is one of the most popular introductions to child development and Waldorf education.

ISBN: 0 85440 352 3   Paper   £4.95

TEACHING AS A LIVELY ART
Marjorie Spock

The author, an experienced Waldorf teacher, conveys her enthusiasm and sense of beauty as she takes us through the various stages of child development.

ISBN: 0 88010 127 X   Paper   £7.50

RUDOLF STEINER EDUCATION AND THE DEVELOPING CHILD
Willi Aeppli

In this book, an experienced Waldorf teacher allows us to enter his classroom — we hear the children speak, we see their faces, and we remember for a while what it was like to be eight years old.

ISBN: 0 88010 164 4   Paper   £7.95

ENCOUNTERING THE SELF: TRANSFORMATION AND DESTINY IN THE NINTH YEAR
Hermann Koepke

The author gives a lucid explanation of events in the life of the child between the ninth and tenth year, a time when the ego incarnates more deeply.

ISBN: 0 88010 279 9   Paper £8.00

ON THE THRESHOLD OF ADOLESCENCE: THE STRUGGLE FOR INDEPENDENCE IN THE TWELFTH YEAR
Hermann Koepke

The approach of adolescence is a worrying time for both children and their parents. This book tells the story of how a young teacher, with the help and guidance of an experienced colleague, coped with the problems and struggles her young students faced as they took their first tentative steps on the road to independence.

ISBN: 0 88010 357 4   Paper £10.95

CHILDHOOD
Caroline Von Heydebrand

This is the classic work on the Waldorf kindergarten. The author worked with Rudolf Steiner at the first school in Stuttgart and her book contains a wealth of insights about working with pre-school children.

ISBN: 0 88010 269 2   Paper £5.50

JOURNEY THROUGH TIME IN VERSE AND RHYME: POEMS COLLECTED BY HEATHER THOMAS FOR TEACHERS OF CHILDREN

This very comprehensive collection of poems, riddles, ballads, birthday verses and prayers gathered over many years is a must for teachers, parents, children and all who love poetry.

ISBN: 0 85440 686 7   Large Format £14.95

UNDERSTANDING CHILDREN'S DRAWINGS
Michaela Strauss

Beautifully illustrated with dozens of children's drawings, this is a thorough, yet easy to follow introduction to art in early childhood.

ISBN: 0 85440 330 2   Cloth   £11.00

ALL OF THE ABOVE TITLES ARE AVAILABLE THROUGH RUDOLF STEINER PRESS. FOR A FREE CATALOGUE OF OVER 350 TITLES, PLEASE WRITE TO:

RUDOLF STEINER PRESS
KIDBROOKE MANSION
MICHAEL HALL
FOREST ROW
EAST SUSSEX RH18 5JB
TEL. No. 0342 825823